Psalm 91 M [...]
provides a cl [...]
the promise [...]
children. M [...]
comfort from Psalm 91, and [...]
the catalyst. This book is pure encouragement, and its fruit will only be fully known in heaven. We have sown the seed, to one army and one marine family with husbands in combat zones in Iraq and to an unbelieving spouse of a naval officer who is now quoting Psalm 91 every day over her children. I have shared it with other naval officers when I was deployed to the Persian Gulf on an aircraft carrier last year. If your ears have become dull to God's promises, get this book and be renewed to a heart of faith in God's provision of protection.

—CAPTAIN HANK BOND
US NAVY

Peggy Joyce Ruth's masterpiece on Psalm 91 captivates your attention. She masterfully helps you face your trials. Military men and women will especially find this book helpful as they face danger. I highly recommend *Psalm 91 Military Edition* by Peggy Joyce Ruth for anyone needing salvation, comfort, healing, protection, or encouragement.

—MAJOR JAMES F. LINZEY
DD CHAPLAIN
US ARMY PRESIDENT, OPERATION FREEDOM

Psalm 91 Military Edition is a well-done, timely message and help to those who are or will be in harm's way and for their loved ones. It is a marvelous, precious promise of God from His Word that has sustained America's troops in times of war and armed conflict down through the ages. It will bless and secure noble warriors today.

—Colonel E. H. Jim Ammerman
(Ret.) US Army

Every soldier who has carried a weapon into combat understands the fear involved. In Psalm 91, God promises to protect us from harm if we rely on Him. Peggy Joyce Ruth's book *Psalm 91 Military Edition* explains those promises in an enlightening way so that everyone can rest in His protection and focus on His mission.

—Major Michael D. Melendez
US Army

Peggy Joyce has done it again. This new edition of her book will inspire you with real testimonies of how God provided His "umbrella of protection" over US military personnel again and again during times of war. Your faith will grow as you read Peggy Joyce's interpretation of Psalm 91 and hear these glorious testimonies!

—Scott Kennedy
Founder and Director,
Operation Prayer Shield

PSALM 91
MILITARY EDITION

PEGGY JOYCE RUTH

CHARISMA
HOUSE

Most CHARISMA HOUSE BOOK GROUP products are available at special quantity discounts for bulk purchase for sales promotions, premiums, fund-raising, and educational needs. For details, write Charisma House Book Group, 600 Rinehart Road, Lake Mary, Florida 32746, or telephone (407) 333-0600.

PSALM 91 MILITARY EDITION by Peggy Joyce Ruth
Published by Charisma House
Charisma Media/Charisma House Book Group
600 Rinehart Road
Lake Mary, Florida 32746
www.charismahouse.com

Unless otherwise noted, all Scripture quotations are from the New American Standard Bible, copyright © 1960, 1962, 1963, 1968, 1971, 1972, 1973, 1975, 1977, 1995 by The Lockman Foundation. Used by permission. (www.Lockman.org)

Scripture quotations marked AMP are from the Amplified Bible. Old Testament copyright © 1965, 1987 by the Zondervan Corporation. The Amplified New Testament copyright © 1954, 1958, 1987 by the Lockman Foundation. Used by permission.

Scripture quotations marked KJV are from the King James Version of the Bible.

Copyright © 2012 by Peggy Joyce Ruth Ministries
All rights reserved

Cover design by Justin Evans
Design Director: Bill Johnson

Visit the author's website at www.peggyjoyceruth.org.

Library of Congress Cataloging-in-Publication Data:
Ruth, Peggy Joyce.
Psalm 91 / Peggy Joyce Ruth. -- Military ed.
p. cm.
Includes bibliographical references.
ISBN 978-1-61638-583-5 (pbk.) -- ISBN 978-1-61638-708-2 (e-book)
1. Bible. O.T. Psalm XCI--Criticism, interpretation, etc.
I. Title.

BS145091st .R87 2012
223'.206--dc23
                    2011049290

Portions of this book were previously published by Charisma House, ISBN 978-1-61638-147-9, copyright © 2010.

While the author has made every effort to provide accurate telephone numbers and Internet addresses at the time of publication, neither the publisher nor the author assumes any responsibility for errors or for changes that occur after publication.

15 16 17 18 19 — 10 9 8 7 6
Printed in the United States of America

CONTENTS

FOREWORD

GENERAL GEORGE C. MARSHALL, US Army Chief of Staff during World War II, once said, "We are building...morale, not on supreme confidence in our ability to conquer and subdue other peoples; not in reliance on things of steel and the super-excellence of guns and planes and bombsights, but on things more potent. We are building it on belief; for it is what men believe that makes them invincible."[1]

During my experience as a chaplain to a battalion of marines in Iraq, I saw firsthand what happens when belief in almighty God floods the hearts and souls of men and women rushing into the teeth of battle. This supreme confidence in God is not foxhole religion or superficial faith. It is a life-changing decision to place oneself completely into the loving hands of Him who is greater than the battlefield.

Such a faith is nowhere more vividly demonstrated than in the words of Psalm 91. For thousands of years the "Soldier's Psalm" has given warriors a reservoir of truth to draw from when the night is dark and the hour is difficult. In this timely companion to this timeless psalm, Peggy Joyce Ruth has made clear and accessible the power of God's promises to those who face the ruination and rubble of war.

For those on the home front, read this book as a practical guide to radical intercessory prayer on behalf of your marine, sailor, soldier, or airman.

For those heroes on the front lines, read this book for strength, hope, courage, and salvation. And as you walk with God through the valley of the shadow of death, may the awesome power of His promises, shared in this book, fill your heart, rule your mind, and shield your life. For, "He who dwells in the shelter of the Most High will abide in the shadow of the Almighty" (Ps. 91:1).

—LIEUTENANT CAREY H. CASH
CHAPLAIN, USN

Introduction

NOTHING COULD HAVE THRILLED my heart more than what recently took place in our hometown with our military. The National Guard men and women, along with their families, had just been honored with a citywide dinner where speeches were made and lengthy good-byes offered. In the midst of all the commotion, I piled stacks of my *Psalm 91* books on my card table and attempted to place one in the hands of each of the military personnel and their families. I had been questioning in my mind all evening how many of the books would be misplaced, laid down, or forgotten in all the excitement.

With a father who served in World War II, a brother and a brother-in-law who each served in the military, and a grandson now serving his country as an Air Force policeman, my heart ached for the opportunity to have our soldiers see the awesome protection covenant from God that is brought to light in this book. I doubted they had paid much attention to what was pushed into their hands during all the celebration. However, as the military buses carrying them to their deployment passed, to my absolute delight and in response to a homemade sign bearing the words "We are praying Psalm 91 for you!" several of the guys in uniform held their books out the bus windows and pointed to their copies of *Psalm*

91: God's Umbrella of Protection. What a relief to know God was already working behind the scenes. They had their promises, and they were ready to go.

These promises can literally save your life. Military history is brimming with stories confirming the power of Psalm 91. In this book we have collected stories and testimonies so you can do your own personal study of the psalm. One man's story in particular illustrates this remarkable protection vividly. When a Pennsylvania lieutenant was accidentally discovered by the enemy while attempting to carry out a very important overseas mission, he immediately placed himself in the hands of God. All he could get out of his mouth was, "Lord, it's up to You now." Before he had a chance to defend himself, the enemy shot point-blank, striking him in the chest and knocking him flat on his back. Thinking he was dead, his buddy grabbed the carbine out of his hands and began blasting away with both guns. When his friend finished, not one enemy was left. Later the lieutenant's sister in Pennsylvania got a letter relating this amazing story: the force of that bullet in the chest had only stunned her brother. Without thinking, he reached for the wound, but instead he felt his Bible in his pocket. Pulling it out, he stared at the ugly hole in the cover. The Bible he carried had shielded his heart. The bullet had ripped through Genesis, Exodus…and had kept going, stopping in the middle of the Ninety-First Psalm, pointing like an arrow at verse 7, "A thousand may fall at your side and ten thousand at your right hand, but it shall not approach you." The lieutenant exclaimed, "I did not know such a verse was in the Bible, but precious God, I thank You for it."[1] This man did not realize this protection psalm even existed (just as it happened in my case) until the Lord supernaturally revealed it to him. Perhaps your protection may not manifest as dramatically as it did with this army lieutenant, but your promise is just as reliable. This study is your chance to learn that Psalm 91 can literally save your life!

I encourage you to mark these scriptures in your own Bible as we go straight through this psalm. This is God's covenant shield of protection for you personally. My prayer is that this edition of Psalm 91 will give you the courage to trust.

Setting the Scene

Sundays were usually a comfort, but not this particular Sunday. Our pastor looked unusually serious that day as he made the announcement that one of our most beloved and faithful deacons had been diagnosed with leukemia and had only a few weeks to live. Only the Sunday before, this robust-looking deacon in his midforties had been in his regular place in the choir, appearing as healthy and happy as ever. Now, one Sunday later, the entire congregation was in a state of shock after hearing such an unexpected announcement. Several of the members became upset with the pastor when he said, "Get out all of your silly little get-well cards and start sending them." But I completely understood the frustration that had initiated the remark. However, little did I know this incident would pave the way to a message that was going to forever burn in my heart. Surprisingly, I had gone home from church that day feeling very little fear, perhaps because I was numb from the shock of what I had heard. I vividly remember sitting down on the edge of the bed that afternoon and saying aloud, "Lord, is there any way to be protected from all the evils that are coming on the earth?" I was not expecting an answer; I was merely voicing the thought that kept replaying over and over in my mind. I remember lying across the bed and falling immediately to sleep, only to wake up a short five minutes later. However, in those five minutes I had a very unusual dream.

In the dream I was in an open field, asking the same question that I had prayed earlier, "Is there any way to be protected from all the things that are coming on the earth?" In my dream I heard these words:

In your day of trouble, call upon Me, and I will answer you.

Suddenly, I knew I had the answer I had long been searching for. The ecstatic joy I felt was beyond anything I could ever describe. To my surprise, instantly there were hundreds with me in the dream out in that open field, praising and thanking God for the answer. It was not until the next day, however, when I heard the Ninety-First Psalm referred to on a tape by Shirley Boone, that I suddenly knew in my heart that whatever was in that psalm was God's answer to my question. I nearly tore up my Bible in my haste to see what it said. And there it was in verse 15, the exact statement God had spoken to me in my dream. I could hardly believe my eyes!

I believe that you who are reading this book are among the many Christians to whom God is supernaturally revealing this psalm. You were the ones pictured with me in my dream in that open field who will, through the message in this book, get your answer to the question, "Can a Christian be protected through these turbulent times?"

Since the early seventies, I have had many opportunities to share this message. I feel God has commissioned me to write this book to proclaim His covenant of protection, especially to the military. May you be sincerely blessed by it.

—PEGGY JOYCE RUTH

Psalm 91
Security for Those Who Trust
in the Lord

He who dwells in the shelter
of the Most High
Will abide in the shadow of the Almighty.
I will say to the LORD, "My refuge and my
fortress,
My God, in whom I trust!"
For it is He who delivers you from the
snare of the trapper
And from the deadly pestilence.
He will cover you with His pinions,
And under His wings you
may seek refuge;
His faithfulness is a shield and bulwark.
You will not be afraid of the
terror by night,
Or of the arrow that flies by day;
Of the pestilence that stalks in darkness,
Or of the destruction that lays
waste at noon.
A thousand may fall at your side,
And ten thousand at your right hand,
But it shall not approach you.

You will only look on with your eyes,
And see the recompense of the wicked.
For you have made the LORD, my refuge,
Even the Most High, your dwelling place.
No evil will befall you,
Nor will any plague come near your tent.
For He will give His angels charge
concerning you,
To guard you in all your ways.
They will bear you up in their hands,
That you do not strike your foot
against a stone.
You will tread upon the lion and cobra,
The young lion and the serpent you will
trample down.
"Because he has loved Me, therefore I will
deliver him;
I will set him securely on high,
because he has known My name.
He will call upon Me,
and I will answer him;
I will be with him in trouble;
I will rescue him and honor him.
With a long life I will satisfy him
And let him behold My salvation."

Chapter

WHERE IS MY
DWELLING PLACE?

He who dwells in the shelter of the
Most High will abide in the shadow
of the Almighty.

—Psalm 91:1

HAVE YOU EVER BEEN inside a cabin with a
big roaring fire in the fireplace, enjoying
the wonderful feeling of safety and security
as you watch a storm going on outside? It is a warm,
wonderful sensation, knowing you are being sheltered
and protected from the storm. That is what Psalm 91 is
all about—shelter.

For men and women serving in the Armed Forces,
shelter takes on a whole new meaning. Lieutenant Carey
H. Cash has been a battalion chaplain to infantry marines.
He was recently chaplain to the president at Camp David.
In Operation Iraqi Freedom, his unit was the first ground

combat force to cross the border into Iraq. In his book, *A Table in the Presence*, he relates the stories from the men with whom he was privileged to serve. In one of these stories, he relates their experiences—as well as their wonder and amazement at what God had brought them through. Each of them had a story to tell of the way God had supernaturally sheltered them from harm in those early days of Operation Iraqi Freedom.

Lieutenant Cash writes: "Early on April 12, as I made my way around Saddam's palace grounds, I felt compelled to keep talking to the men and listening to their stories. I sensed in them a deep need, even a compulsion, to articulate their wonder and amazement at what God had brought them through. And this wasn't true of only a handful of Marines. From the youngest private to the oldest veteran, every man seemed to have a story to tell.... Their stories seemed to have one common thread—they all believed they had been in the midst of a modern-day miracle. As they told me what they had seen, their eyes lit up, and their faces glowed.

"It was clear to me that I wasn't merely in the company of warriors, but of witnesses....As they spoke, with tears in their eyes and bullet holes through their clothes, I realized that I too was a witness. These were not men who had 'found religion' momentarily, or who were courteously acknowledging the practical aspects of prayer or faith in times of need. These were men who had stumbled onto something historic...a story that had to be told."[1]

Just as these people experienced a surreal sense of history when they captured Saddam's palace, they also realized that even more had happened. When someone steps out and believes God at His Word, *something historic* does take place, and this book tells those stories. There is a place in God, a secret place, an eternal place for those who want to seek refuge. It is a personal revelation of a literal place of physical safety and security that God tells us about in this psalm. When I think of protection, I think of one particular childhood memory. I remember the peace and security I felt as a young girl after a day of perch fishing with my family. The day was beautiful when we drove the boat across the lake to a secret cove, but suddenly in the middle of the lake the sky turned black, lightning flashed, and drops of rain soon escalated into hailstones. We had no time to get back to the boat dock. Dad quickly drove the boat to an isolated island in the middle of the lake, ordered us onto the shore to lie down on the ground, and quickly covered us with a canvas tarp then crawled under where all five of us lay covered in our makeshift tent. I can remember wishing the storm would last forever. There was a certain calm under that shelter that is still hard to explain. I didn't want anything to spoil the security I felt that day in our secret hiding place, feeling my father's protective arms around me—I never wanted it to end.

Our heavenly Father has a *secret place* in His arms that protects us from the storms that are raging in the world around us. Andrew Wommack was deployed in Vietnam from January 1970 through the end of February 1971, serving in the 196th Infantry Brigade as an assistant to the chaplain. He says that he was well aware of the security God had provided through His protection covenant of Psalm 91 and knew it was just as reliable in wartime as in peacetime. He tells of one experience when he was protected in the secret place of God's shelter right in the midst of a firefight with the Viet Cong.

"I was driving from Da Nang to my headquarters some sixty miles south. It was a paved highway that went north and south through Vietnam. Sometimes people drove alone, but it was against regulations and was especially dangerous when one drove through towns because there were people everywhere. You were forced to slow down almost to a stop with this sea of people around your vehicle, and it was not uncommon for one of them to wrap a cloth around a hand grenade, pull the pin, and throw it into the gas tank. The gas would eat the rag away, releasing the handle and blowing up the gas tank. I had been a little apprehensive about getting through, so my faith was just a little shaky. I specifically remember going across a huge bridge right outside of the town, because I remember I was praying and singing praises to God for His divine protection in getting me through safely.

"I also remember hearing a lot of gunfire, but I didn't think much about it because gunfire was quite common. That was just something you learned to live with. But then as I continued south on Highway One, in less than ten minutes after crossing the bridge, I saw a convoy and another chaplain's assistant who was a friend of mine going north. I waved at him and went on. Later I met this same guy in Da Nang, and he said, "How did you get across the bridge right outside that town?" I said, "I just drove across it. Why?" Then he told me that by the time they got to the bridge, less than ten minutes after I had crossed it, the convoy was stopped because of all the bodies of Vietnamese and Americans they had piled up who had been killed. It turned out the Viet Congs had been on one side of the bridge, the Americans on the other side, and while I was just singing and worshiping the Lord, I had driven over the bridge, right through the middle of the firefight. I was totally unaware I was driving through a huge gunfire battle, and I never got touched. 'A thousand may fall at your side and ten thousand at your right hand, but it shall not approach you' (Ps. 91:7)."[2]

That secret place is literal, but it is also conditional. In verse 1, God lists our part of the condition before He even mentions the promises included in His part. That's because our part has to come first. To abide in the shadow of the Almighty, we must first *choose to dwell* in the shelter of the Most High.

The question is, "How do we dwell in the security and shelter of the Most High?" It is more than an intellectual experience. It is a dwelling place where we can be physically protected if we run to Him. You may utterly believe that God is your refuge; you may give mental assent to it in your prayer time; you may teach Sunday school lessons on this concept of refuge; you may even get a warm feeling every time you think of it; but unless you do something about it—*unless you actually get up and run to the shelter*—you will never experience it.

You might call that place of refuge—a *love walk!* In fact, the secret place is, in reality, the intimacy and familiarity of the presence of God Himself. When our grandchildren Cullen and Meritt, ages ten and seven, stay the night with us, the moment they finish breakfast, each runs to his own secret place to spend some time talking with God. Cullen finds a place behind the divan in the den, and Meritt heads behind the lamp table in the corner of our bedroom. Those places have become very special to them.

There are times when your secret place may have to exist in the midst of crisis circumstances with people all around you. A good example of that is a situation in which a US Navy boy from Texas found himself. Running spiritually to his secret place is most likely what saved his ship from disaster.

He and his mother had decided to both repeat Psalm 91 each day at a given time to add agreement to his protection covenant. He later told of a time when his ship was under attack from the air and from an enemy submarine at the same time. All battle stations on the ship were in operation when the sub came within firing range and loosed a torpedo directly toward them. At that moment the young man realized it was the exact time that his mother would be saying Psalm 91, so he began quoting the psalm just as the torpedo's wake appeared, heading directly toward their battleship. However, when it was just a short distance away, it suddenly swerved, passing the stern and disappearing. But before the men had time to rejoice, a second torpedo was already coming straight toward them. "Again," he said, "as the second torpedo got almost to its target, it suddenly seemed to go crazy, causing it to turn sharply and pass by the bow of the ship. And with that, the submarine disappeared without firing another shot."

The whole ship must have been "under the shadow of the Almighty" because it didn't receive as much as a scratch from either the submarine or the planes flying overhead.[3]

Where is your secret place? You too need the security and shelter of a secret place with the Most High.

Chapter

WHAT IS COMING OUT OF MY MOUTH?

I will say to the LORD, "My refuge
and my fortress, my God, in whom I
trust!"

—Psalm 91:2

NOTICE THAT VERSE 2 says, "I will say." Circle
the word *say* in your Bible because we must
learn to verbalize our trust aloud. Basically
we answer back to God what He said to us in the first
verse. There is power in saying His Word back to Him!
We are not told to simply think the Word. We are told
to say the Word. For example, Joel 3:10 tells the weak to
say, "I am a mighty man." Over and over we find great
men of God such as David, Joshua, Shadrach, Meshach,
and Abednego declaring their confessions of faith aloud
in dangerous situations. Notice what begins to happen
on the inside when you say, "Lord, You are my refuge,

You are my fortress, You are my Lord and my God! It is in You that I put my total trust!" The more we say it aloud, the more confident we become in His protection.

So many times as Christians we mentally agree that the Lord is our refuge, but that is not enough. Power is released in saying it aloud. When we say it and mean it, we are placing ourselves in His shelter. By voicing His Lordship and His protection, we walk through the door to the secret place.

One cannot miss the fact that this verse uses the word *my* three times: "my refuge…my fortress…my God!" The psalmist makes a personal claim to God. The reason we can trust is because we know who God is to us. This verse makes the analogy of who God is; He is a refuge and a fortress. These metaphors are significant military terms. God Himself becomes the defensive site for us against all invading enemies. He is personally our protection.

Have you ever tried to protect yourself from all the bad things that can happen? God knows we cannot do it. Psalm 60:11 tells us, "Deliverance by man is in vain." God has to be our refuge before the promises in Psalm 91 will ever work.

We can go to the doctor once a month for a checkup. We can double-check our cars every day to make sure the motor, the tires, and the brakes are all in good working order. We can fireproof our houses and store up food for a time of need. We can take every precaution imaginable that the military offers, yet we still could not do enough to protect ourselves from every potential danger life has to offer. It is impossible.

It isn't that any one of these precautions is wrong. It is that not one of these things, in and of itself, has the power to protect. God has to be the One to whom we run first. He is the only One who has an answer for whatever might come.

When I think of how utterly impossible it is to protect ourselves from all the evils in the world, I am reminded of sheep. A sheep has no real protection other than its shepherd. In fact, it is the only animal I can think of that has no built-in protection. It has no sharp teeth, no offensive odor to spray to drive off its enemies, no loud bark, and it certainly cannot run fast enough to escape danger. That's why the Bible calls us God's sheep. God is saying, "I want you to see Me as your source of protection. I am your shepherd." (See John 10:11.) Now, we may use doctors, protective military/police equipment, or bank accounts to meet our specific needs, but our hearts have to run to Him first as our shepherd and our protector. Then He will choose the method He desires to bring about the protection.

Some quote Psalm 91 as though it were some magical wand, but there is nothing magical about this psalm. It is powerful, and it works simply because it is the Word of God, alive and active. We confess it aloud simply because the Bible tells us to.

When I am facing a challenge, I have learned to say aloud, "In this particular situation (name the situation aloud) I choose to trust You, Lord." The difference it makes when I proclaim my trust aloud is amazing.

Take notice of what flies out of your mouth in times of trouble. Crystal Phillips, mother of Jeff Phillips, a corporal in the United States Marine Corps serving on board the USS *Bonhomme Richard*, one of seven warships sent to Iraq in the early months of Operation Iraqi Freedom, tells a story that demonstrates the importance of speaking repeatedly of our faith in God and His promises of protection. Jeff continually spoke of his tremendous faith, direction and encouragement for his family to stand strong, and of the peace and assurance he was receiving—even from the war zone—as he read God's Word, including Psalm 91. His faith (and his family's) was tested soon after the start of the war. His mother tells the story.

"Seven days following the declaration of war my husband and I received a large brown envelope in the mail from the state senator's office. The address on the envelope was handwritten to us. Inside was a letter signed and stamped with the senator's official seal. It was a letter bearing an evil report, offering condolences for the loss of our son.

"Scanning over the first few lines brought me to a crisis of belief. Knowing that I am not a particularly strong person in my own strength, I look back now and find that I am quite amazed at the way I responded. Without God and the assurance of His promises, I know that I would have crumbled. My first response was, 'This is a mistake, and I will not believe this evil report!' I at first thought that I would ignore it and throw the letter away. Then I realized that I had to continue to declare God's promises that are written in Psalm 91. I thought, 'I have to call the senator's office to let them know about this mistake so other errors like this will be avoided.' Making that call led to a long wait for a response, but I refused to spread the evil report. My daughter-in-law called, but I did not tell her. I did not even call my husband. For approximately two hours I paced through my house, vocally fighting a spiritual battle by loudly declaring the promises of God's Word. Some may disagree, not seeing the urgency of such action, but I knew that I had to line my thoughts, my confessions, and my agreement up with God's Word. I knew that my son's life was on the line! The devil had devised a plan to take my son's life, and I had no choice but to stand in the gap. I could not agree with the 'evil report.' The letter was a tool to cause me to give up my confession of faith so the enemy could gain the access that he desired.

"The blood of Jesus and the miraculous power and protection of God that is unlimited by time or distance are what placed my son under the shadow of His almighty wings. I would not give the enemy entry! Doubters might ask if I believe that the outcome could have been different! My answer to that is a definite yes! My son was in and out of foxholes, while dodging rounds of fire that were falling inches from his feet. Had I placed my agreement with the enemy and lost my will to trust, pray, declare, and believe God, my son might not be here today.

"Finally the phone rang with a profuse apology and

confirmation that the letter had been sent by mistake. At that point I called and shared the experience with my husband, assuring him that 'all is well.' Still months passed before we heard the voice of our son. I could never adequately describe how wonderful it was on that Thursday in June, around two in the morning, when we heard Jeff say, 'What's up? I am in Germany waiting to fly to California. Can you book me a flight to Dallas on Friday night, and will you pick me up?'"[1]

Our part of this protection covenant is expressed in verses 1 and 2, "He who dwells" and "I will say." Psalm 91 tells us to speak life!

C. B. Morelock, a war correspondent in World War II, reported an unexplainable and miraculous occurrence: sixty German aircraft strafed more than four hundred men who were pinned down on the sandy Dunkirk beaches without the benefit of anyplace to take cover. Although the men were repeatedly attacked by machine guns and bombed by enemy aircraft, not one single man was hit. Every man *in that group* left the beach without a scratch. Morelock stated, "I have personally been told by Navy men who picked up those particular survivors from Dunkirk, that the men not only recited Psalm 91, *but they shouted it aloud at the top of their lungs!*"[2] Saying our trust aloud releases faith! It releases God's power to bring about His amazing promises in verses 3 through 16, which we will look at in the following chapters.

Chapter

TWO-WAY DELIVERANCE

For it is He who delivers you from
the snare of the trapper and from the
deadly pestilence.

—Psalm 91:3

HAVE YOU EVER SEEN a nature program in
which a fur trapper travels deep into the
mountains in the cold climate? He baits big
steel traps, covers them over with branches, and then
waits for some unsuspecting animal to step into the
trap. Those traps were not there by chance. The trapper
has taken great care in placing them in very strategic
locations. In wartime a minefield is set up the same way.
Land mines are methodically placed in well-calculated
locations.

These are pictures of what the enemy does to us. That
is why he is called the trapper! The traps that are set
for us are not there by accident. It is as if the trap has
your name on it. They are custom made, placed, and

baited specifically for each one of us. But like an animal caught in a trap, it is a slow, painful process. You don't die instantly. You are ensnared until the trapper comes to destroy you.

I will never forget a tragedy that happened to a good friend of mine whose husband was stationed with the military overseas. Having quit in the middle of numerous career possibilities, requiring a number of expensive moves, the young man finally joined the army without consulting anyone, including his wife. It was hard on this young wife who had faithfully undergone countless abrupt alterations and changes of direction in her way of life. However, she was very supportive and constantly defended her husband's behavior.

Unfortunately his low self-esteem and immature conduct left him wide open for the enemy's trap. He had been so accustomed to giving in to his flesh that when the enemy placed a beautiful and willing young girl in front of him, he temporarily forgot the faithful young wife back home who had supported him through so much. That was the straw that broke the camel's back. It is not repetitive to say, "Hurting people hurt people." This couple got caught in a downward spiral. Her years of pain and self-sacrifice left her hopeless, and the marriage could never be restored. Because the couple was ignorant of the schemes of the enemy, the trap that he so carefully laid accomplished exactly what it was sent to accomplish. The bait was set at the exact moment the husband was most vulnerable to fall.

The enemy knows exactly what will hook us, and he knows exactly which thought to put into our minds to lure us into the trap. That is why Paul tells us in 2 Corinthians 2:11, "So that no advantage would be taken of us by Satan, for we are not ignorant of his schemes [traps]." Then he says:

> For the weapons of our warfare are not of the flesh, but divinely powerful for the destruction of fortresses. We are destroying speculations and every lofty thing raised up against the knowledge of God, and we are taking every thought captive to the obedience of Christ.
>
> —2 Corinthians 10:4–5

God not only delivers us from the snare laid by the trapper (Satan), but according to the last part of verse 3, He also delivers us from the deadly pestilence. I always thought a pestilence was something that attacked crops—bugs, locusts, grasshoppers, spider mites, mildew, and root rot. After doing a word study on the word *pestilence*, I found that it attacks people, not crops. A *pestilence* is any deadly disease or condition that attaches itself to one's body with the intent to destroy. But in Psalm 91:3 God says that He will deliver you from the deadly disease (pestilence) that comes with the intent to destroy.

Natalie Ogletree, a financial manager and an employee at the Pentagon at the time of 9/11, tells a miraculous story that demonstrates God's deliverance from the snare of the trapper and the deadly pestilence.

When the plane smashed into the building, she was at her job on the fifth floor in the adjacent wedge of the impact. Since the ceiling in front of her office had collapsed, she and coworkers were directed to an emergency exit route at the rear of the office. She gathered up her things and started for an exit. Thinking they were trapped, one can only imagine their relief when they finally found the fire escape that delivered them straight to the ground floor.

When the group of about twenty-five coworkers arrived at the first floor, military personnel were desperately running to the impact site, retrieving wounded persons, and bringing them to a secure area where they could be laid on the floor and their injuries could be attended to. Natalie was on her way out of the building with her coworkers when she came across a military man who was being carried by several men. When she looked over, something told her to let her group go on and for her to return to this particular man. He was severely injured with burns over 60 percent of his body, but he was not dead. However, his body looked not only burned but injured as well. As a child, Natalie had fallen into a bucket of hot water that her mom was using to mop the floor, so she knew what it was like to have burns from her knees to her shoulders. She still had scars and could remember the pain.

The man's shoes had blown off, his socks were gone, his arms and face were burned, and his whole body was smoky and charred. He was screaming for relief from the pain. She ran to his side, and he asked Natalie to make sure she would call his wife, Mel, and tell her he was OK. Every indication was that he was not going to make it, so Natalie listened carefully to the words to give to his wife. Several times it appeared that he was slipping away because the pain and injuries were so severe.

As the military performed triage on him, Natalie held his hand and prayed with him, trying to get his mind off the pain. She began to quote the Lord's Prayer and Psalm 23. However, there was a psalm that three weeks before, her mother, Delores Green, had told her about—Psalm 91. In fact, her mother had asked Natalie to pray it every morning. She was glad that she had grabbed her Bible that was lying on her desk beside her purse in the haste. Natalie did not know the psalm by heart, but miraculously two flips and she was there. She began to read the words.

"He who dwells in the shelter of the Most High will abide in the shadow of the Almighty…!" She began to declare Psalm 91 over him. She would later find out the injured man was Colonel Brian Birdwell. Colonel Birdwell's arms were bloody and his feet were still smoking, but she read this psalm of protection over him. Then she would return to Psalm 23, which she knew by heart, and would quote it with him, and they would pray the Lord's Prayer. Then back to Psalm 91. For thirty to thirty-five minutes she went back and forth at least seven times reading the psalm over him.

Something supernatural was taking place in him. She prayed with him one more time and told him, "You are going to be OK!" She exited, but God was still not finished. Once she was out of the building, she ran into him again and could see the extent of his injuries, so she prayed once again.

There were no ambulances that could make it into the Pentagon, so those in charge were trying to wave down civilians to transport the injured. They loaded him into a small SUV, but it was not large enough, and they took him back out again. Only a few vehicles behind that car was an army captain in a Ford Expedition who took him to Georgetown University Hospital. Natalie continued to pray. She had done everything she knew to do in the natural, and it didn't look good, but she had activated the supernatural power of God's Word over him. For two months she searched for any information about him and kept her church and her Bible study praying for him. Then, on December 2 or 3, she heard on the news about a survivor's miraculous story—and she began to cry, knowing in her heart that it was Colonel Birdwell.

Later the next spring Natalie would meet someone in the Pentagon who asked her if she had met someone on September 11. The gentlemen informed her, "Brian is looking for you!" Natalie and her family (Mark, Avery, and Aaron) would eventually meet Lieutenant Colonel Brian Birdwell, his wife, Mel, and their son, Matthew. It was not until the anniversary of the Pentagon attack that she realized that the date 9/11 was just like the psalm she had read.

Natalie's mother had been very timely in telling her daughter about Psalm 91 just three weeks before this traumatic event. And in this life-and-death situation, that advice helped to save a life as Natalie stood on these promises of Psalm 91 for over half an hour. This was a man whom no one expected to live until someone took the time and risked their own safety to bring God's Word into the tragedy. When Colonel Birdwell needed the encouragement to keep fighting to live, it wasn't his military training that kicked in—it was the prayers and the Word that Natalie Ogletree brought to him in that critical moment.[1]

As a soldier, there are enemies that attack your mind (thoughts), some attack your body internally (germs), and some attack with weapons (people). This is your verse, insuring your deliverance from all the varieties of harm. Thank God for His deliverance from traps and pestilence.

Chapter

UNDER HIS WINGS

He will cover you with His pinions, and
under His wings you may seek refuge.
—PSALM 91:4

WHEN YOU PICTURE A magnificent flying
bird, it is usually not a chicken that comes
to mind. I've never seen a chicken pictured
in flight—many eagles, but no chickens. We quote the
scripture from Isaiah 40:31 that talks about being borne
up on the wings of eagles or with wings like eagles.
There is a difference, however, between being "on" His
wings and being "under" His wings. This promise
in Psalm 91 is not elaborating on the flying wing but
on the sheltering wing. One indicates strength and
accomplishment, while the other denotes protection
and familiarity. When you picture the warmth of a
nest and the security of being under the wings of the
nurturing love of a mother hen with chicks, it paints a

vivid picture of the sheltering wing of God's protection that the psalmist refers to in this passage.

Is everyone protected under the wings? Did you notice that it says He will cover you with His pinions (feathers), and under His wings you may seek refuge? Again, it is up to us to make that decision. We can seek refuge under His wings if we choose to.

The Lord gave me a vivid picture of what it means to seek refuge under His wings. My husband, Jack, and I live out in the country, and one spring our old mother hen hatched a brood of baby chickens. One afternoon when they were scattered all over the yard, I suddenly saw the shadow of a hawk overhead. I then noticed something very unique that taught me a lesson I will never forget. That mother hen did not run to those little chicks and jump on top of them to try to cover them with her wings. Instead she squatted down, spread out her wings, and began to cluck. And those little chickens, from every direction, came running to her to get under those outstretched wings. Then she pulled her wings down tight, tucking every little chick safely under her. To get to those babies, the hawk would have to have gone through the mother.

When I think of those baby chicks running to their mother, I realize it is under His wings that we may seek refuge, but we have to run to Him. "He will cover you with His pinions, and under His wings you may seek refuge." That one little word, *may*, is a strong word. It is up to us. All that mother hen did was cluck and expand her wings to tell them where to come:

Jerusalem, Jerusalem....How often I wanted to
gather your children together, the way a hen gathers
her chicks under her wings, and you were unwilling.
—Matthew 23:37

Notice the contrast between His willingness and our
unwillingness, His wanting to against our not willing
to, His would against our would not. What an unbeliev-
able analogy to show us theologically there is protection
offered that we don't accept.

It is interesting that Jesus uses the correlation of
maternal love to demonstrate His attachment to us.
There is fierceness to motherly love that we cannot
overlook. God is deeply committed to us, yet at the
same time, we can reject His outstretched arms if we so
choose. It is available, but it's not automatic.

Captain Nick Cataechis served with the Army
Transport Unit with 150 other soldiers, delivering
supplies on the road between the Baghdad Airport and
Abu Ghraib in Iraq in 2004. These men ran to God
each morning for protection by praying the words of
Psalm 91 before their missions. Kay Gibson, cofounder
of Houston Marine Moms, tells how this became their
daily strategy for God's protection.

"About a year ago I met this army mom, Judith Cook,
who was helping her son's unit—the 15th Transportation
Unit from Fort Sill, Oklahoma—get ready to deploy to
Iraq three days after Christmas 2004. Judith's son Nick is
a captain of the Army Transport Unit, with 150 soldiers in
this unit. The commander's wife contacted Judith and told

her this group delivers supplies on the road between the Baghdad Airport and Abu Ghraib; therefore, they were expecting extremely high casualties. She was wondering if Judith would start making a quilted banner with a gold star in memory of each soldier they expected to be killed in action or severely injured. Judith asked what sort of casualty rate they were expecting. She was told 50–75 percent! On the Internet Judith found some camouflage bandanas with the Ninety-First Psalm printed on them. The Ninety-First Psalm is considered the *psalm of protection* for our troops. Judith hand-delivered these bandanas to the soldiers in this unit and *made them promise to say this psalm every day before their missions*. Every day both the officers and soldiers would say this psalm together.

"During the deployment Nick's unit was attacked on an almost-daily basis with IEDs and mortars, as well as snipers. There were countless stories of mortars that never detonated, mortars that exploded nearby, but no shrapnel injuries to Nick's group, no ambushes on their Humvees, and no injuries.

"In one incident several of Nick's men were in the mess hall when a mortar exploded less than twenty feet away. Shrapnel was all around, yet none of the soldiers were injured. There was an attack on the army buildings where the soldiers sleep, and three of the buildings were damaged, but the mortar that landed on top of Nick's building was a dud. Several of Nick's men were in a PX near Baghdad when it was attacked. Everyone in the PX was injured—except Nick's men. Nick sent the following e-mail describing these incidents:

> We got hit again really bad night before last in three separate engagements. We received small arms fire on the first two, and another explosive on the third. I've attached a photo of the vehicle that took most of the blast. Remarkably, other than a possible concussion and some ringing ears, no one was hurt seriously. This armor we have is really good stuff. Unfortunately we've had the chance to try it out on more than one occasion, but at least we know it is good stuff. We had a mortar attack also on the same day. One of the guys was outside working and heard a really loud noise and had rocks thrown on him. He looked over and saw an unexploded mortar lying on the gravel about 8–10 feet from him. Needless to say, he took off running. *If you are praying for us, it must be working. That's the only explanation of how no one has been seriously injured yet.*—Nick

"Day after day these soldiers gathered to pray this psalm together. In December 2005, after almost a year in Iraq, Nick and his unit returned home—all 150 soldiers. They did not lose ONE soldier, nor were any of them injured! THE POWER OF PRAYER IS AWESOME!"[1]

God does not run here and there, trying to cover us. God has made protection possible if we run to Him. And when we do run to Him in faith, the enemy will have to go through God to get to us. What a comforting thought!

Chapter

A MIGHTY FORTRESS
IS MY GOD

His faithfulness is a shield and
bulwark.

—Psalm 91:4

I T IS GOD'S FAITHFULNESS to His promises that is
our shield. It is not solely our faithfulness. God is
faithful to the promises He has made.

When the enemy comes to whisper fearful or
condemning thoughts in your mind, you can ward off
his attack by saying, "My faith is strong because I know
my God is faithful, and His faithfulness is my shield!"

How often I've heard people say, "I cannot dwell in
the shelter of God. I mess up and fall short too many
times. I feel guilty and unworthy." God knows all about
our weaknesses. That is why He gave His Son. We can
no more earn or deserve this protection than we can
earn or deserve our salvation. The main thing is if we

slip and fall, we must not stay down. Get up, repent, and get back under that shield of protection. Thankfully this verse says it is His faithfulness, not ours, that is our shield.

> If we are faithless, He remains faithful, for He cannot deny Himself.
>
> —2 TIMOTHY 2:13

Our daughter slipped and fell facedown in the busiest four-way intersection in our city. Embarrassment made her want to keep lying there so she did not have to look up and show her face to so many people who would know her in a small town. However, the worst thing she could have done was to lie there! This is a humorous illustration of what it looks like when we fall. When you think of her lying facedown in that busy intersection, don't ever forget that the worst thing you can do after you fall spiritually is fail to get up!

This verse just expresses again God's commitment and faithfulness to being our shield of protection. It is His faithfulness that gets us back on our feet and moving again. His unshakable faithfulness is a literal shield. I have an awesome mental picture of a huge shield out in front of me, completely hiding me from the enemy. The shield is God Himself. His faithfulness to His promises guarantees His shield will remain steadfast and available forever, but whether or not we stay behind that protection is our choice.

This scripture also tells us God's faithfulness is our bulwark. According to *Nelson's Bible Dictionary*, "a bulwark is a tower built along a city wall from which defenders shoot arrows and hurl large stones at the enemy."[1] Think about that! God's faithfulness to His promises is not only a shield, but it is also a tower. From that tower God is faithful to point out the enemy so he cannot sneak up on our blind side. *Webster's New World Dictionary* defines the word *bulwark* as "an earthwork or defensive wall, fortified rampart; a breakwater; the part of a ship's side above the deck."[2] If you are on board a ship, the word *bulwark* gives you a visual of His protection.

Throughout history there have been shields over individuals and groups who have stood on Psalm 91. Probably the most famous one is from World War I. On both sides of the Atlantic religious and secular publications reported the story of a "miracle regiment" who went through some of the most intense battles without a single combat casualty. The best sources say it was a British-American unit rather than exclusively an American one. Our researchers have enjoyed rebuilding this bridge between the event and its sources and uncovering new leads to one of the most celebrated pulpit examples of the power of Psalm 91. The story says that every officer, as well as enlisted men, recited the Ninety-First Psalm together, and that unit is known to have suffered not one single combat casualty. The division was engaged in three of the bloodiest battles of World

War I: Chateau Thierry, Belleau Wooe, and Argonne. Other units engaged in those same battles had up to 90 percent casualties. There are still some unanswered questions regarding this story, but it keeps reappearing with World War I vets who brought home a testimony about Psalm 91.

When Marian Jones was cleaning the mantle in her home in Arkansas, she saw something wedged in an artillery shell her father, Lieutenant Harry McGee Cooper, had brought home from World War I. It was his Psalm 91 testimony written out and stuffed inside the shell that had *Argonne 1918* engraved on it—the actual battle scene of this famous story. That shell had been on the mantle for as long as Marian could remember, and the ability to hear the story from her father had died with him years earlier. So many of the great Psalm 91 stories are still being discovered and need to be told. It is unthinkable to believe mere chance or coincidence could have prevented so many bullets and shells from finding their intended victims.[3]

Dunkirk, in World War II, is another prime example. During the dreadful yet heroic week in May of 1940, when the British army had been forced into total retreat and lay exposed on the sandy shores of Dunkirk, many miracles occurred. Lying hopelessly exposed, pinned down by Nazi planes and heavy artillery, and armed only with their rifles, the brave troops were seemingly trapped by the channel with no place to turn for protection. A British chaplain told of lying facedown in the sand for what seemed an eternity on the shell-torn beach at Dunkirk. Nazi bombers dropped their lethal charges, causing shrapnel to kick up sand all around him while other planes repeatedly strafed his position with their machine guns blazing.

Although dazed by the concussions around him, the British chaplain suddenly became aware that, in spite of the deafening roar of the shells and bombs falling all around him, he had not been hit. With bullets still raining down about him, he stood and stared with amazement at the outline of his own shape in the sand. It was the only smooth and undisturbed spot on the entire bullet-riddled beach. His heavenly shield must have fit the exact shape of his body.[4]

Note that Psalm 91:4 declares God's faithfulness to us as both a shield and a bulwark. He is using two military symbols of fortification and protection. He is our tower, our wall of protection in a collective sense, and our shield, a very personal piece of protective gear. This verse is indicating double protection.

Chapter

I WILL NOT FEAR THE TERROR

> You will not be afraid of the terror by night.
>
> —Psalm 91:5

PSALM 91:5 COVERS AN entire twenty-four-hour period by emphasizing God's protection over both day and night. But most importantly, these two verses encompass every evil known to man.

The psalmist divides the list into four categories. We will look at those categories one at a time. The first, terror by night, includes all the evils that come through man: kidnapping, robbery, rape, murder, terrorism, and wars. It is the dread, horror, or alarm that comes from what man can do to you. God says that you will not be afraid of any of those things because they will not approach you. The first thing this verse deals with is not being afraid.

Over and over Jesus told us, "Do not fear!" Why do you think He continually reminds us not to be afraid? Because it is through faith in His Word that we are protected, and since fear is the opposite of faith, the Lord knows fear will keep us from operating in the faith that is necessary to receive. It is no wonder God addresses the fear and terror first.

In Psalm 91 God gives us instructions to quiet the fear that rises in our hearts. These words, "You will not be afraid of the terror by night or of the arrow that flies by day," are addressing the anxiety that comes the night before battle. Fear is never more prevalent than in wartime. Men have wrestled with this fear in many different ways. After a commanding officer confessed to his men that he experienced fear before every battle, one of his soldiers asked him, "How do you prepare for battle?" The officer took out his Bible, opened it, and showed him Psalm 91.

Fear comes when we think we are responsible for bringing about this protection ourselves. Too often we think, "Oh, if I can just believe hard enough, maybe I will be protected!" That's wrong thinking! The protection is already there. It has already been provided, whether we receive it or not. Faith is simply the choice to receive what Jesus has already done. The Bible gives classic examples of how to deal with terror.

The answer is in the blood of Jesus. Exodus 12:23 tells us when Israel put blood on the door facings, the destroyer could not come in. The animal blood they used then served as a type and shadow, or a picture, of the blood of Jesus that ratifies our better protection under our better covenant. (See Hebrews 8:6.)

When we confess aloud, "I am protected by the blood of Jesus," and believe it, the devil literally cannot come in. Remember, Psalm 91:2 tells us, "I will say to the LORD, 'My refuge and my fortress.'" It is heart and mouth—believing with our heart and confessing with our mouth.

Our physical weapons are operated with our hands, but we operate our spiritual weapons with our mouths. The blood is applied by saying it in faith. Confessing with our mouth and believing with our heart starts with the new birth experience and sets precedence for receiving all of God's good gifts. (See Romans 10:9–10.)

If we find ourselves being afraid of the terror by night, that is our barometer letting us know we are not dwelling and abiding up close to the Lord in the shelter of the Most High and believing His promises. Fear comes in when we are confessing things other than what God has said. When our eyes are not on God, fear will come. But let that fear be a reminder to repent.

For we walk by faith, not by sight.
—2 CORINTHIANS 5:7

We have to choose to believe His Word more than we believe what we see and more than we believe the terror attack. It's not that we deny the existence of the attack, for the attack may be very real. But God wants our faith in His Word to become more of a reality to us than what we see in the natural.

For example, gravity is a fact. No one denies the existence of gravity, but just as the law of aerodynamics can supersede the law of gravity, Satan's attacks can also be superseded by a higher law—the law of faith and obedience to God's Word. Faith does not deny the existence of terror. There are simply higher laws in the Bible for overcoming it.

David did not deny the existence of the giant. Fear has us compare the size of the giant to ourselves. Faith, on the other hand, had David compare the size of the giant to the size of his God. David's eyes saw the giant, but his faith saw the promises. (See 1 Samuel 17.)

Can you imagine the terror you would feel having to make a crash landing during World War II and then learning that you are on an island occupied by Japanese soldiers? This next story is a perfect example of being delivered from the terror by night. When one of our bombers, returning after a successful mission, ran out of gas, the crew members were forced to land on the sandy beach of a Japanese-occupied island, several hundred miles from base.

"Chaplain, now is your chance to prove what you have been preaching," the men chided. "You have been telling us for months that we must pray and God will deliver us from the terror all around us. We need a miracle now." The chaplain began fervently praying, and the first thing they noticed was that their landing had gone unnoticed by the enemy. Night fell, and he continued to pray.

About 2:00 a.m. they heard a new sound on the beach side, and in spite of the terror that was looming over the group, they crept to the water's edge so silently that they didn't even disturb the chaplain, who was still kneeling in prayer. They were able to make out the dim outline of a large barge, but no voices or footsteps could be heard aboard. If the crew was asleep, there was no sentry on the deserted deck. Aboard the barge, the deck was covered with oil drums filled with high-octane gasoline. They could hardly restrain a shout of joy. It seemed like a dream. This drifting barge had brought them the one thing in all the world that could get their bomber off the island and back to the home base. They ran back across the sand and embraced their startled chaplain, used their in-flight refueling hose, and thunderously took off down the beach runway.

A later investigation revealed that the skipper of a US tanker, after finding himself in submarine-infested waters, had ordered his gasoline cargo removed to lessen the danger from a torpedo hit. Barrels of gasoline were placed on barges and set adrift—some six hundred miles from where the bomber had landed. In just a few weeks that oil barge had aimlessly drifted the whole six hundred miles across the Pacific and beached just fifty steps from the stranded men—all within twelve hours of their crash.[1] The chaplain's prayers had been heard, and they were delivered from the terror by night.

We do not have to be afraid of the terror of what man can do to harm us. There is not a way in the world to escape this terror unless God's higher law comes into effect. God promises triumph over man's worst devices. If applied, this is incredible assurance.

Chapter

I WILL NOT FEAR THE ARROW

> You will not be afraid...of the arrow
> that flies by day.
>
> —Psalm 91:5

THE SECOND CATEGORY OF evil is the arrow that flies by day. An arrow is something that pierces or wounds spiritually, physically, mentally, or emotionally. Arrows are intentional. This category indicates you are in a spiritual battle zone where specific enemy assignments are directed toward your life to defeat you. Arrows are deliberately sent by the enemy and meticulously aimed at the spot that will cause the most damage. They are targeted toward the area where our mind is not renewed by the Word of God, perhaps an area where we are still losing our temper, or an area where we are still easily offended, or perhaps an area of rebellion or fear. Very seldom does the enemy attack us in an area where we are built up and strong. He attacks us where we're still struggling. That's why we have to resist and not get lazy spiritually. God tells us in Ephesians 6:16 we have a "shield of faith...to extinguish all the flaming arrows of the evil one [enemy]."

This covers the area of intentional danger. Someone bends the bow and pulls back the bowstring. The arrows are aimed and released. These are not regular, everyday arrows; they are on fire. God doesn't say we can miss most of them. He says we can extinguish "all" of them. When arrows are sent to wound us spiritually, physically, mentally, emotionally, or financially, God wants us to ask and believe by faith that He will pick us up out of harm's way and deliver us from calamity.

Sergeant George Harold Barclay served in World War II in General Patton's 320th Infantry of the US Army, Company E. Continuous fear eliminated any expectation of ever returning to his wife and baby daughter. The same fear kept his wife terrified whenever she would see a Western Union truck delivering letters of war casualties. Once a Western Union messenger came to her door by mistake, and she said she froze with terror. Sometimes as many as six weeks would go by without a letter from her husband, during which time the news reported that half of Barclay's company had been killed. The Battle of the Bulge saw his whole outfit cut off from the rest of the army.

Finally, however, a letter came from Harold saying that God had given him Psalm 91, and he now had absolute certainty that he would come home without even an injury. So certain was he of this promise in Psalm 91 that when the medics said they needed volunteers to go to the front lines to bring back the injured, Harold volunteered and made repeated trips under extreme enemy fire, saving many lives.

The citation for the Bronze Star he received said, "For bravery," but Harold insisted it was not bravery since he knew nothing would happen to him because of the covenant promise God had given to him in Psalm 91. When he came home without a scratch, it was obvious that *he was not afraid and was delivered from the arrows that fly by day.*[1]

We have a covenant with God, telling us not to be afraid of the arrow that flies by day. Assignments will rise up, but don't be afraid of the arrows. He has promised they will not hit their target.

Chapter

I WILL NOT FEAR
THE PESTILENCE

[You will not be afraid] of the
pestilence that stalks in darkness.
—PSALM 91:6, EMPHASIS ADDED

FEAR GRIPPED MY HEART and beads of perspiration popped out on my forehead as I feverishly ran my fingers over what felt like a lump in my body. How I dreaded the monthly self-examination that the doctor had suggested. My fingertips were as cold as ice from the panic I had worked up just thinking about what I might find and the turn my life might take from there. On that particular day it turned out to be a false alarm, but the dread of what I might find in the coming months was constantly in the back of my mind until this promise came alive in my heart. If you fight fears of fatal diseases, then this is the scripture for you to take hold of.

The third category of evil God names is pestilence. This is the only evil He names twice! Since God does not waste words, He must have a specific reason for repeating this promise.

Have you noticed that when a person says something more than once, it is usually because he wants to emphasize a point? God knew the pestilence and the fear that would be running rampant in these end days. The world is teeming with fatal epidemics hitting people by the thousands, so God catches our attention by repeating this promise.

It's as though God is saying, "I said in verse 3, 'You are delivered from the deadly pestilence,' but did you really hear Me? Just to be sure, I am saying it again in verse 6, 'You do not have to be afraid of the deadly pestilence!'" This is so contrary to the world that we have to renew our thinking. Only then can we comprehend the fact that we do not have to be afraid of the sicknesses and diseases epidemic in the world today.

When I first started studying this psalm, I remember thinking, "I don't know whether I have the faith to believe these promises!" This thought stretched my faith and my mind until I thought it would snap like a rubber band that was being pulled too tightly.

God, however, reminded me that faith is not a feeling. Faith is simply choosing to believe what He says in His Word. The more I chose to believe God's Word, the more I could trust and rely on it completely.

Our inheritance is not limited to what is handed down to us genetically from our ancestors. Our inheritance can be what Jesus provided for us if we believe the Word and put it to work.

> Christ redeemed us from the curse of the Law, having become a curse for us.
>
> —GALATIANS 3:13

The pestilence mentioned here in Psalm 91 is spelled out in detail in Deuteronomy 28. This scripture in Galatians tells us we are redeemed from every curse (including pestilence) if we will believe and appropriate the promise.

Never before in our history has there been so much talk of terrorism and germ warfare, but to the surprise of so many people, God is not shocked or caught off guard by these things. Do we think chemical warfare is bigger than God? Long before man ever discovered biological weapons, God had made provision for the protection of His people, if they would believe His Word.

> These signs will accompany those who have believed...if they drink any deadly poison, it will not hurt them.
>
> —MARK 16:17–18

The word *drink* in this scripture comes from the Greek word for "imbibe,"[1] which means "to drink, to absorb, to inhale or to take into the mind."[2] No evil has been conceived by man against which God has not provided a promise of protection for any of His children who will choose to believe it and act on it.

What about the fear that has come on mankind regarding our polluted water supplies or foods contaminated by pesticides? I believe the Word of God advocates using wisdom, but all the precautions in the world cannot protect us from every harmful thing that could be in our food and water. Therefore God's instruction to bless our food and water before eating is not simply some ritual to make us look more spiritual. Rather, it is another provision for our safety, playing an important role in God's protective plan.

> But the Spirit explicitly says that in later times... men [will]...advocate abstaining from foods which God has created to be gratefully shared in by those who believe and know the truth. For everything created by God is good, and nothing is to be rejected if it is received with gratitude; for it is sanctified by means of the word of God and prayer.
> —1 TIMOTHY 4:1–5

> But you shall serve the LORD your God, and He will bless your bread and your water; and I will remove sickness from your midst.
> —EXODUS 23:25

It is God's goodness that made these provisions before we ever asked! This is not for everyone; it is for those who believe and know the truth. Blessing the food with gratitude literally brings about sanctification, or a cleansing of our food and water.

In Bible days when they mentioned pestilence, they were thinking of diseases like leprosy. Luke 21:11 states that one of the signs of the End Times is an outbreak of pestilence. Today there are many widespread diseases such as AIDS, cancer, malaria, heart disease, and tuberculosis, to name a few, but no matter what pestilence we might be facing, His promise never ceases to be true.

Rene Hood experienced the reality of this promise twenty years after her service in the US Army. In July 1998 she began suffering with devastating physical symptoms. Several months later, after seeing her VA nephrologist, she was told, "You are in the last stages of lupus and are going to die. I give you three months, and you will just go 'poof.'" After twelve long days in the hospital, she took a stand on God's promise to *believe for her miracle* and went to her parents' home to wait for her healing. It took agonizing months of persistence in claiming the promises of Psalm 91 and every healing scripture she could fine, but the miracle finally manifested! After a CAT scan and two sonograms, the doctors could find no mass on her liver and told her she was "a miracle." A blood specialist confirmed that she was "a wonder." She has seen many Christmases since being told she would not live to see that 1998 Christmas. Rene is active in prison ministry and even took a mission trip with us to very remote areas of the Philippines. She has never had a relapse.[3] God's Word is true no matter what the circumstances look like at times.

I shudder to think what we might open ourselves up to without the promise of Psalm 91 and without the determination to stand firm and refuse to entertain fearful thoughts. What we allow our mind to dwell on is our choice. Therefore if we desire to operate in this protection covenant, taking authority over negative thoughts and emotions is imperative. It is amazing how the simple phrase "I am just not going there" will dispel those fear thoughts immediately.

I am sure this promise of protection from plagues and pestilence reminded the Jews of Israel's complete immunity from the Egyptian plagues in the land of Goshen. The destroyer could not come in where the blood was applied. Even in this Old Testament psalm God has declared that we will not be afraid of the pestilence that stalks in darkness; it will not approach us.

Chapter

I WILL NOT FEAR THE DESTRUCTION

[You will not be afraid] of the
destruction that lays waste at noon.
—Psalm 91:6

THIS FOURTH CATEGORY OF evil is destruction. Destruction includes the evils over which mankind has no control. Those are the things the world ignorantly calls "acts of God," such as tornadoes, floods, hail, hurricanes, and fire. God very plainly tells us we are not to fear destruction. These natural disasters are not from God.

In Mark 4:39 Jesus rebuked the storm, and it became perfectly calm. This demonstrates God is not the author of such things; otherwise, Jesus would never have contradicted His Father by rebuking something sent by Him.

There is no place in the world where you can go and be safe from every destruction and natural disaster. We can never anticipate what might come when we least expect it. But no matter where you are in the world, God says to run to His shelter where you will not be afraid of the destruction—it will not approach you!

Our granddaughter, Jolena, and her husband, Heath Adams, US Air Force, were stationed in Turkey right before the war was declared in Iraq. Soon after her arrival in Turkey, Jolena started working as a lifeguard at a pool. While at work one day at the end of June, she began to hear a loud noise that sounded much like a plane breaking the sound barrier; then everything started to shake. Everyone around her began to panic when the water splashed in the pool from an earthquake she later found to be a 6.3 on the Richter scale. Swimmers were desperately trying to get out of the water to find a place of safety, and children clung to Jolena and screamed in fear. People everywhere were hollering, but Jolena said she felt a peace and a calm come over her. She started praying in a loud voice, pleading the blood of Jesus over the air force base and the people there. Suddenly everyone around her became perfectly quiet and began listening to her pray. No one on the base was seriously hurt, but just five minutes from there, apartment buildings had collapsed and more than one thousand people were killed in the quake. Heath was at work as he watched the wall of a building completely crumble and fall to the street.

Every day Jolena and Heath had been praying Psalm 91 protection over their home, and it certainly paid off.

The base had a great deal of structural damage. The post exchange (PX) and the gym were completely lost, and many of the houses were destroyed. Not only were houses destroyed, but furniture, TVs, and stereos were ruined as well, causing hundred of thousands of dollars of damage. Many of the houses had such huge cracks from the earthquake you could actually see through the walls. One block from their home, a staircase had completely separated from the wall. Their miracle was that, other than one tiny crack over one of the doorways, there was not one bit of damage to their house or to any of their furnishings. While many of their friends had to move out of their homes so they could be repaired, Jolena and Heath did not have to go through any of that. God wants us to take seriously His promise that we do not have to fear destruction and that it will not approach us.

Did you know that every extreme evil known to man will fall into one of these four categories in verses 5–6: terror, arrows, pestilence, or destruction? The amazing thing is that God has offered us deliverance from them all!

God has said in His Word we will not be afraid of terror, arrows, pestilence, or destruction—they will not approach us—if we are obedient to verses 1 and 2 to dwell in His shelter and abide in His shadow. This psalm is not filled with exceptions or vague conditions, as if trying to give God an out or an excuse to fail to fulfill the promises. Rather, it is a bold statement of what He wants to do for us.

We can receive anything God has already provided. The secret is knowing that everything for which God has made provision is clearly spelled out and defined in the Word of God. If you can find where God has offered it, you can have it! God will never hold it back. His provision is already there, waiting to be received.

In 1966 Rick Johnson decided to drop out of college and join the Marine Corps so he could go to Vietnam. The Marines were looking for pilots and wanted him to go to flight school, but he was determined to be a grunt (infantry).

He completed his training and got orders to go to Vietnam just as he had requested. Just before leaving home, his fiancée's mother, Erma Carroll, asked him to sit down so she could read something to him. She read Psalm 91 and told him how much it meant to her and that the Lord had put it on her heart to read that scripture to him before he left. He was not familiar with that section of Scripture, but he remembered where it was and read it from time to time. One experience in Vietnam illustrates God's protection over Rick. He tells the story.

"In the spring of 1967, the lonely combat base at Khe Sanh, just south of the demilitarized zone (DMZ) and not far from the border of Laos, was like most other places in Vietnam, unknown to the world. (Not for long.) We landed at the airstrip and were immediately ordered to join a number of other Marine companies strung along the narrow footpaths. Our job was to search through the rugged mountainous terrain for the North Vietnamese Army units who had been assigned to wipe Khe Sanh off the map.

"Our first day out we were approaching hill 861. I was stepping over the bloated body of a Marine, thinking something is very wrong. (Marines never leave anyone behind. For this body to be lying exposed on a lonely, recently burned and blasted hill was more than wrong. I had never seen this before. We all knew something was up and were 'beyond' fully alert.) Just then the North Vietnamese Army (NVA) opened fire on us. I carried the PRC-25 radio for the platoon leader, who was immediately in front of me. In the initial volley of fire, the lance corporal in front of the lieutenant was hit badly, and the man behind me had his left arm shattered. The primary target in the initial volley of an ambush is to take out the radio man and the man next to him (communications and leadership). There was no doubt in my mind who had been in the gunner's sights when he pulled the trigger. I rolled left and the lieutenant rolled right as we dove for cover that simply did not exist. We had just passed the crest of a hill that had been hit with napalm, leaving less than two inches of grassy stubble. We were exposed. We both scrambled back to allow the top of the small hill to provide a semblance of cover. The company commander wanted a report, so I passed the handset to the lieutenant. The lead elements of our platoon were cut off from us in a deep, steep ravine, dividing the hill where the enemy was concealed in bunkers from the hill we were on. Our staff sergeant, who was with the other group, organized an assault and had all the men pull the pin on grenades, ready to storm the hill in front of us. Our rocket launcher team (headed up by a Christian) was beside the lieutenant and me, fully exposed, effectively firing on the enemy positions. When out of rocket ammunition, the team leader yelled to the wounded lance corporal in front of us who still lay fully exposed to the enemy, 'I'm coming to get you.' With that, we all started firing ferociously with our rifles to cover our buddies, and all three of our machine gunners appeared and stood fully erect, shoulder to shoulder, firing from the hip to cover this heroic rescue. This is the most beautiful sight anyone could ever hope to have etched in his memory. I can still see the smoke, fire, and brass spewing from these guns as the wounded man was carried, arms and legs dangling, over the top of the hill to a waiting corpsman who would tend to his multiple wounds.

"A little later, I found myself still pinned down talking on the radio behind a 'log' that was about eight inches in diameter. Another buddy piled in on top of me, wanting to get into one more good fight before he left for home. I described to him what he would see when he looked up and that the most accurate fire was from the bunker just to the right of the small, lone tree across from us. Not realizing that the gunner was still trying to take me out (since I had the radio) and that he was, at that moment, sighted in on my radio antenna that stuck up from my position, my friend raised his head to look. Three shots

from the enemy's automatic weapon hit him in the forehead about an inch below the rim of his helmet, and he
fell lifeless onto me. He saved my life with that move. He
didn't do it on purpose, but he saved my life. I was just
through talking on the radio and was getting ready to do
exactly what he had just done that cost him his life."

Corporal Ira "Rick" Johnson saw more than two
hundred combat days with Third Battalion, Ninth
Marine Regiment, Third Marine Division in the
Republic of Vietnam from August 1966 until September
1967 and has been awarded the Bronze Star, the Purple
Heart, and several other medals for combat service
while serving in the Marine Corps.[1] If there was ever
a need for protection from destruction, it was what the
soldiers went through in the Vietnam War. This is such
an important promise for those serving in our military
with our current military challenges.

God is faithful to all the promises He has made. He
did not create man and then leave man to himself. When
He created us, He automatically made Himself responsible to care for us and meet our every need. When He
makes a promise, He is faithful to what He has promised. This psalm seems to build from one promise to the
next. Men are judged by their faithfulness to their own
word. Real men are only as good as their word. God is
more faithful than even the most truthful man, for He
has the power to carry out His Word.

Chapter

THOUGH A THOUSAND FALL

> A thousand may fall at your side and
> ten thousand at your right hand, but it
> shall not approach you.... For you have
> made the LORD, my refuge, Even the
> Most High, your dwelling place.
>
> —PSALM 91:7, 9

DO WE EVEN STOP to consider what this is saying to us? Do we have the courage to trust God's Word enough to believe He means this literally? And is it possible for it to be true and yet still miss out on these promises? Jesus makes this same point about unclaimed promises when He said in Luke 4:27, "There were many lepers in Israel in the time of Elisha...and none of them was cleansed." Only Naaman the Syrian was healed when he obeyed in faith. Not everyone will receive the benefits of this promise in

Psalm 91. Only those who believe God and hold fast to His promises will profit; nonetheless, it is available. To the measure we trust Him, we will in the same measure reap the benefits of that trust.

What an awesome statement! God wants us to know that even though there will be a thousand falling by our side and ten thousand at our right hand, it does not negate the promise that destruction will not approach the one who chooses to believe and trust His Word. One translation reads, "It shall not come near you *[for any purpose]*" (Ps. 91:7, AMP). God means exactly what He says.

It is no accident that this little statement is tucked right here in the middle of the psalm. Have you noticed how easy it is to become fearful when disaster starts striking all around you? We begin to feel like Peter must have felt as he walked on the water to Jesus. It is easy to see how he started sinking with the waves when he saw all the turbulence of the storm going on around him.

John Marion Walker, a survivor of the Bataan Death March of World War II and the three-and-a-half-year imprisonment as a prisoner of war that followed, knows the reality of this promise. On the same day Pearl Harbor was bombed, John heard his name called three times, and finally he got off his cot and went to see what his buddy wanted. A bomb fell right into his cot and exploded. The buddy was incredulous. He had never called John's name. This would be only the beginning of the events that took place to spare his life. Seventy-five thousand prisoners began that march—but only one in three survived to go home. John lost 100 pounds during that sixty-mile forced march—going from 165 pounds to 65 pounds. His boots wore out and he survived the years as a POW barefoot. On January 26, 1945, after years of cruel, forced slave labor, he was moved to his final destination. Barefoot and wearing only underwear, the men were forced to walk in hip-deep snow to Prison Camp Wakasen, Japan, where they worked in the lead and zinc mine as slave labor for seven months. Once when the mine caved in, God supernaturally showed John a ladder that had not been there before, and all were able to make it to safety. On another occasion he survived four blows to the head by a six-inch by six-inch timber. When the war was finally over, John returned home—alive because of God's supernatural protection that kept him alive against all physical odds imaginable. And John found out his brother had prayed Psalm 91 over him the entire time he was at war.[1]

Many who were taken prisoner with John Walker did not survive. God knew there would be times when we would hear so many negative reports, see so many needs, and encounter so much danger around us we would feel overwhelmed. That is why He warned us ahead of time that thousands would be falling all around us. He did not want us to be caught off guard. But at that point we have a choice to make. The ball is then in our court! We can either choose to run to His shelter in faith, and it will not approach us, or we can passively live our lives the way the world does, not realizing there is something we can do about it.

Psalm 91 is the preventive measure that God has given to His children against every evil known to mankind. Nowhere else in the Word are all of the protection promises (including help from angels and promises ensuring our authority) accumulated in one covenant to offer such a total package for living in this world. It is both an offensive and defensive measure to ward off every evil before it has had time to strike. This is not only a cure, but it is also a plan for complete prevention.

What tremendous insight, after the Word of God has renewed our minds, to realize that, contrary to the world's thinking, we do not have to be among the ten thousand who fall at our right hand.

> You will only look on with your eyes and see the recompense of the wicked.
>
> —PSALM 91:8

You will see some recompense (payment) at times being doled out. There is judgment. Every sin will be exposed sooner or later and paid for. An evil dictator falls, an unrighteous aggressor is stopped, a tyrant faces his crimes against humanity, a wrong is rectified—the recompense of the wicked speaks of justice. Wars have been fought where one side had a righteous cause, and consequently, good won over evil. The justness of God is that evil will not triumph…that the Hitlers of the world do not win…that communistic governments fall…that darkness does not extinguish light.

This verse says that we will "only look on and see" it happening. The word *only* denotes a protection of only seeing and not experiencing the evil, and it denotes detachment in that the evil we see does not get inside of us. We are set apart in that we do not allow our enemy's hate to change us.

Let's look for just a moment at this scripture with our faith in mind—do we sometimes fall short into unbelief?

Faith in God, in His Son Jesus Christ, and in His Word is counted in God's eyes as righteousness. But when we are in unbelief, to a degree we are placing ourselves in the category of the wicked. Sometimes, even as a Christian, I have been an unbelieving believer when it comes to receiving all of God's Word.

Jesus says in Matthew 5:18, "Not the smallest letter or stroke shall pass from the Law until all is accomplished." Even if believers have never utilized this psalm in its full potential, the truth has never passed away or lost one ounce of its power.

Many people think of the gospel as an insurance policy, securing only their eternity or their comfort if disaster strikes. They are depriving themselves of so much. Perhaps we all need to ask ourselves the question, "What kind of coverage do I have, fire or life?" God's Word is more than merely an escape from hell—it is a handbook for living a victorious life in this world.

There is a difference between the destruction of the enemy and persecution for the gospel's sake. Second Timothy 3:12 tells us, "All who desire to live godly in

Christ Jesus will be persecuted." There are times when we will be mistreated because of our stand for the cause of Christ. Psalm 91 is a very distinct concept dealing with natural disasters, accidents, sickness, and destruction. Jesus suffered persecution, but He was not plagued by calamity, disaster, or mishap. Accidents never even approached Him. This distinction is easy to understand if you separate persecution from freak accidents and mishaps.

There is a place where calamity literally does not even approach us. This would be seemingly impossible to imagine—especially in combat situations. Yet to look at this verse with thousands falling on either side in its true context, we observe the strongest description of casualty and calamity named in the psalm. If this verse isn't a description of actual combat, I don't know what is—and yet, tied to it, is a promise of protection beyond anything that could be envisioned. This portrayal of people falling is directly connected to the promise that it will not even come near us. Two opposite poles joined together!

Too many people see Psalm 91 as a beautiful promise that they file right alongside all of their other good quality reading material, and it makes them feel comforted every time they read it. But I do not want anyone to read this book and fail to see the superior significance to these promises in this psalm. These are not written for our inspiration but for our protection. These are not words of comfort in affliction but words of deliverance from affliction.

Chapter

NO PLAGUE COMES
NEAR MY FAMILY

> No evil will befall you, nor will any
> plague come near your tent.
> —Psalm 91:10

ARE YOU WORRIED ABOUT your family at home?
This part of Psalm 91 is written just for you.
After God repeats our part of the condition in
verse 9, He then reemphasizes the promise in verse 10:

Nor will [it] come near your tent [your household].

It is at this point in the psalm that the Bible makes
this covenant more comprehensive than merely being
about ourselves. God adds a new dimension to the
promise: the opportunity to exercise faith not only
for ourselves but also for the protection of our entire
household.

If these promises were only available to us as

individuals, it would not be completely comforting. Because God has created within us both an instinct to be protected and a need to protect those who belong to us, He has assured us in this verse that these promises are for you and your household.

It appears that the Old Testament leaders had a better understanding of this concept than we who are under the new covenant. That is why Joshua chose for himself and for his household.

> If it is disagreeable in your sight to serve the LORD, choose for yourselves today whom you will serve…but as for me and my house, we will serve the LORD.
> —JOSHUA 24:15

As Joshua made the decision that his household would serve God with him, he was influencing their destiny and declaring their protection at the same time. In much the same way, Rahab bargained with the Israeli spies for her whole family. (See Joshua 2:13.)

When our hearts are truly steadfast and we trust in His faithfulness to fulfill His promises, we will not constantly be afraid something bad will happen to one of our family members.

> He will not fear evil tidings; his heart is steadfast, trusting in the LORD.
> —PSALM 112:7

One of my most memorable experiences was when I had the privilege of speaking to some of the residents of Seadrift, Texas, and heard them tell stories of God's magnificent protection over their soldiers during World War II. A group of mothers and friends in their hometown of Seadrift fervently prayed for their safety daily until they returned. Pictures of the fifty-two soldiers were placed in a large picture frame at the church and prayed over daily. Everyone I interviewed was still excited to tell me, "All fifty-two came home!" Every Seadrift soldier returned safely from the battlefields of Europe, the South Pacific, and the Far East, in spite of the fact that hundreds of thousands of American lives were lost on those battlefronts.

One of these praying mothers, Fanny Maude (Granny) McCown, was quite a prayer warrior. Known as a Five-Star Mother for having five sons in World War II at the same time, she could often be heard crying out through tears as she prayed aloud in the family's smokehouse for the protection of her boys. Scattered throughout the world, those young men blessed practically every branch of the service. Glen McCown was in the army and fought in the Pacific theater. Danger faced him every day of the war as he had the perilous job of going into caves throughout the islands looking for Japanese. Eugene McCown served in the navy in the South Pacific and was a constant target while operating landing crafts to lay down ground troops. Milton actively served in the navy, as well, throughout the war.

Another of Fanny McCown's sons, Gerald, joined the air force and fought in Europe. He was sent overseas in the largest convoy to ever cross the Atlantic Ocean, and they were forced to travel in total blackout at night to be undetected by the enemy. Gerald McCown experienced the protective hand of God on numerous occasions. Some of his vivid memories were the times when he helped drop supplies from an airplane to ground troops in England and France as he stood on top of a thick steel plate because bullets came up through the bottom of the plane. Gerald said they would often fly behind enemy lines and drop supplies and food to General Patton and his ground troops to help keep them moving as rapidly as possible across Europe to stop the Nazi advancement.

Hollis McCown, another of Fanny's sons, never left the States but knew his job of servicing the planes to keep them in optimum shape for our fliers and refueling them for their important missions was a vital link in the success of the war. Her sixth son entered World War II after the declaration was signed, then later fought again in the Korean War. What a heritage Fanny Maude McCown and her family have left for their descendants.

The incredible story of God's protection did not end with World War II. Gerald's grandson, Sergeant Leslie King, while serving in Germany, showed *The 700 Club* documentary of the miracle at Seadrift to his church there, trying to encourage other churches to do the same. In Iraq, King carried on the legacy of his grandfather and uncles, and the church in Seadrift has continued in the famous heritage left to them.

Sergeant King believed strongly in the power of prayer and took comfort in the fact that he knew his church back home was praying. He had written home describing the shield of protection he felt around himself and around all of his men in Iraq, but suddenly, the feeling of security and safety that he had been experiencing was gone, and he felt vulnerable and apprehensive. From there everything started going wrong. Two of his friends were killed along with some others, and for a period of time their food and water were being rationed. Then, to make matters worse, his time in Iraq was extended by four more months.

He called his mother to say that something was not right. He didn't feel the shield of protection anymore for his men, and everything seemed to be going wrong. It was at that time the family noticed all the military pictures were gone from the bulletin board. They had been taken down because the actual "war" was considered to be over. (Little did anyone know the battles yet to be fought!) After this was brought to the attention of the pastor, the photos were put back. Interestingly, without knowing that his picture had been removed and subsequently put back on display, Sergeant King wrote home again to say that his peace and security had returned. They didn't lose any more men, and the troubles had begun to subside. The family knew that it was no coincidence that the deaths and trouble occurred within the three-week period when the photos were out of sight. Even though the troops were being prayed for, there was something about the pictures being displayed and the church members having visual contact when they prayed, that made a big difference. What a powerful tool prayer is![1]

In Matthew 13:31–32, Jesus makes reference to the mustard seed starting as an herb but growing into a tree with the birds nesting in the branches. Others can find protection in our faith as well when we plant the seed of the Word.

When old-timers were asked about the population of the town, it seemed that everyone had a family member who had gone to fight. What a testimony to this promise of family protection when every single man returned home from war—from all over the world. *This town did not suffer a single combat casualty* while so many other towns and families experienced much grief and heartache and, many times, multiple casualties! This is one of the many reasons why this psalm is known as "The Soldier's Prayer."

The same is true for you. The beauty of this psalm is that when someone prays for more than himself, he brings the entire family under the shield of God's Word. It is an added dimension to us as individuals to be able to apply the richness of this covenant for our entire household. Many support groups of wives, mothers, and sisters have evolved to pray for the soldiers in the field. What a joy to know you have promises in Psalm 91 that will protect not only you but also those in your family and near your dwelling as well.

Chapter

ANGELS WATCHING OVER ME

> For He will give His angels charge concerning you, to guard you in all your ways. They will bear you up in their hands, that you do not strike your foot against a stone.
>
> —Psalm 91:11–12

HERE IN VERSES 11–12 God makes another unique promise concerning an additional dimension of our protection. This is one of the most precious promises of God, and He put it right here in Psalm 91. In fact, this is one of the promises Satan used to test Jesus in the wilderness.

Most Christians read past this promise with very little, if any, thought about the magnitude of what is being said. Only after we get to heaven will we realize all the things from which we were spared because of the intervention of God's angels on our behalf.

I am sure you have read stories about missionaries whose lives were spared because would-be murderers saw large bodyguards protecting them when, in fact, there was no one there in the natural. The same is true with soldiers who have had similar experiences in combat. We all can remember close calls in which we escaped a tragedy and there was no explanation in the natural. Not only is it possible "[to entertain] angels without knowing it," as it says in Hebrews 13:2, but sadly, I believe most Christians have a tendency to disregard the ministry of angels altogether.

Several famous writers, including C. S. Lewis, have alluded to the battle at Mons, Belgium, where a great number of the British soldiers reported having seen what they all called an intervention by angels who came to their aid against the Germans in August 1914. According to the reports of these soldiers, this angelic assistance could not have come at a more perfect moment as they were being overrun by persistent German advancement. There is a similar version of the Mons story told by German prisoners who described what they called an army of ghosts armed with bows and arrows and led by a very tall figure on a white horse who urged the English troops to go forward. Many diaries and letters show that by 1915, the British had accepted the belief that a supernatural event had indeed taken place. Military historians who have studied this Belgium battle scene have enthusiastically incorporated the appearance of the angels at

Mons into their writings. In another account of the battle in Mons some Coldstream Guards who were the last to withdraw had become lost in the area of the Mormal Forest and had dug in to make a last stand. An angel appeared and led them across an open field to a hidden, sunken road that enabled them to escape. England has had a long history of linking the heavenly to the military.[1]

Dorothy Geer, grandmother of Lance Corporal Christopher Stevenson, USMC, wrote to tell me of the times when her grandson experienced angelic protection while on duty in a Humvee in Iraq in 2003. She wrote:

Christopher left for Iraq on August 25, 2004. While praying for him on September 3, 2004, when I got to verse 11 of Psalm 91 the Lord showed me a picture in my mind's eye of Christopher on guard duty, and God's angels were guarding him. Shortly after that, on one of Christopher's first patrols (he was a machine gunner on top of a Humvee), his truck hit a land mine and it did not explode! He said it was a double-stacked, anti-tank land mine. On another patrol his Humvee hit a land mine that exploded and destroyed the truck, but all of the men walked away unhurt! The Lord showed me that when I prayed verse 12 over Christopher, it was protection from land mines.

Near the end of his deployment, he was in a firefight at night. The enemy (unseen because it was night) was firing a machine gun directly at Christopher. He was returning fire at the flashes he could see each time the insurgent's weapon was fired. He told me he really thought he would die that night because he could see the tracers from the weapon coming close by his head. All of a sudden the insurgent stopped firing. Christopher was not sure if it was because he hit him or if he ran out of ammunition, but Christopher began singing out loud on top of that Humvee, "Lord, I Lift Your Name on High." That so touched my heart because Christopher knew it was God who saved him. He had written John 15:13 on a card and taped it near his machine gun, "Greater love has no one than this, that one lay down his life for his friends." Not too many civilians know this, but the gunner on top of the Humvee is known in the Marine Corps as the guardian angel. It is up to the gunner to protect his fellow marines in the truck and keep watch for the enemy all around. It is a very dangerous position, and if the enemy cannot blow up the truck, they try to at least take out the gunner. Praise God for His covenant of protection, Psalm 91.

Most sincerely, Dorothy Geer

P.S. Christopher also prayed Psalm 91 over himself and his men before they went out on patrol.[2]

Are you in harm's way? Do you feel alone? You are not alone. He has given His angels—personal heavenly bodyguards—to protect you. There are more fighting for you than against you.

Verse 11 of Psalm 91 says, "For He will give His angels charge concerning you." What does that mean? Think with me for a moment. Have you ever taken charge of a situation? When you take charge of something, you put yourself in a place of leadership. You begin telling everyone what to do and how to do it. If angels are taking charge of the things that concern us, God has given the angels, not the circumstances, the authority to act on our behalf. That same truth is repeated in Hebrews:

> Are they [angels] not all ministering spirits, sent out to render service for the sake of those who will inherit salvation?
>
> —HEBREWS 1:14

When we look to God as the source of our protection and provision, the angels are constantly rendering us aid and taking charge of our affairs. Psalm 103:20 says, "…His angels, mighty in strength…obeying the voice of His word!" As we proclaim God's Word, the angels hasten to carry it out.

Psalm 91:11 also says "Angels…[will] guard you in all your ways." Have you ever seen a soldier standing guard, protecting someone? That soldier stands at attention: alert, watchful, and ready to protect at the first sign of attack. How much more will God's angels stand guard over God's children, alert and ready like bodyguards to protect them at all times? Do we believe that? Have we even thought about it? Faith is what releases this promise to work on our behalf. How comforting it is to know God has placed these heavenly guards to have charge over us.

Psalm 91 names so many different avenues through which God protects us. It is exciting to realize from this Old Testament psalm that protection is not just an idea in God's mind; He is committed to it. Angelic protection is another one of the unique ways in which God has provided that protection. What an unusual idea to add actual beings designed to protect us. He has charged angels to guard us in all our ways.

Chapter

THE ENEMY UNDER
MY FEET

> You will tread upon the lion and
> cobra, the young lion and the serpent
> ["dragon" in KJV] you will trample
> down.
>
> —PSALM 91:13

HERE IN VERSE 13 God takes us from the subject of our being protected by Him and emphasizes the authority in His name that has been given to us as believers. Make a note of the corresponding New Testament scripture dealing with the authority that has been given to us:

> Behold, I [Jesus] have given you authority to tread
> on serpents and scorpions, and over all the power of
> the enemy, and nothing will injure you.
>
> —LUKE 10:19

We as Christians have been given authority over the enemy. He does not have authority over us. We need to take the time to allow that fact to soak in! However, our authority over the enemy is not automatic.

My husband believes that too few Christians ever use their authority. Too often they pray when they should be taking authority! For the most part, Jesus prayed at night and took authority all day. Encountering the enemy is not the time to start praying—we need to be already prayed up. When we encounter the enemy, we need to speak forth the authority we have in the name of Jesus.

If a gunman suddenly faced you, would you be confident enough in your authority that you could boldly declare, "I am in covenant with the living God, and I have a blood covering that protects me from anything you might attempt to do. In the name of Jesus, I command you to put down that gun!"

If we do not have that kind of courage, then we need to meditate on the authority scriptures until we become confident in who we are in Christ. At new birth we immediately have enough power placed at our disposal to tread upon the enemy without being harmed. Most Christians, however, either do not know it or they fail to use it. How often do we believe the Word enough to act on it?

Now let's look at what this verse is actually saying. What good does it do to have authority over lions and cobras unless we are in Africa or India or some place like that? What does it mean when it says that we will tread on the lion, the young lion, the cobra, and the dragon?

This is a graphic illustration of things that are potentially harmful in our daily lives. These terms are just an unforgettable means of describing the different types of satanic oppression that come against us. So, what do these terms mean to us today? Let's break them down.

First of all, there are "lion problems." These problems are bold, loud, and forthright and come out in the open to hit us head-on. At one time or another we have all had something blatant and overt come against us. It might have been a car wreck or a face-to-face encounter with the enemy on the battlefield. It might have been an unexpected bill at the end of the month causing a chain reaction of bounced checks. Those are lion problems, obvious problems that often seem insurmountable. Yet God says we will tread on them; they will not tread on us.

The "young lions" can grow into full-grown problems if we don't handle them. These young lion problems come to harass and destroy us gradually. Subtle negative thoughts that tell us we will not survive, that our mate no longer loves us, or that we are no longer in love with our mate are good examples of this category. Those young lion problems can grow into big ones if they are not taken captive and destroyed. (See 2 Corinthians 10:4–5.) Answer them with the Word of God. Small harassments, distractions, and irritations are young lions.

Next, God names "cobra problems." These are the problems that seem to sneak up on us like a snake in the grass throughout our day while we're minding our own business. They are what we might call an undercover attack that brings sudden death—a deceptive scheme keeping us blinded until it devours us. A surprise military ambush, failure to distinguish the enemy from a civilian, and a "Dear John" letter are examples of cobra problems. Thank the Lord we have authority to tread over such things so these surprise attacks will not overpower us.

On July 30, 2009, Brian Spears, a National Guard soldier with Georgia's 48th Brigade serving in Afghanistan, was traveling in a military caravan headed to Kabul to await a flight out of the country to begin his R&R (rest and recuperation). Before they left, the caravan had prayed Psalm 91, and without knowing it, they were about to experience God's protection from a "cobra attack." His MRAP vehicle was hit by an IED that was packed in a culvert pipe running underneath the road. The vehicle was thrown six to eight feet in the air. They later learned that the culvert was packed with more than twelve hundred pounds of explosives and set off a shock wave felt more than one mile back. The pressure from the blast was so powerful that it even broke the watch on Brian's wrist. The hands of the watch froze. One man commented, "Time seemed to stand still at this moment." All that remained was a gaping hole the entire width of the roadway—but God had saved the lives of all the men in that vehicle!

In September of that same year, Brian and his unit had finished their tasks and gathered like a football huddle for the Psalm 91 prayer. Oddly, after loading the MRAP, they were called back for paperwork errors and put off schedule. They began exiting the base in Ghazni when they saw a man lying in the middle of the street and profusely bleeding. He had been riding a motorcycle and was hit by an oncoming vehicle. The convoy did not stop to assist the man because of their late departure. About 1.8 miles down the road, they heard an explosion and learned that the man they had just passed was a suicide bomber who had planned to detonate his bomb as the convoy passed. As the last vehicle in the convoy pulled safely into the base, another explosion was heard. They learned this was another Taliban suicide bomber who had planned to set off his bomb as the convoy rolled into base, which caused an error in the timing of the explosive. Not one soldier in any convoy was killed from either explosion, which would have had caused heavy casualties. Brian said, "If we had rolled out at the scheduled time, then there is no doubt that this day would have drastically changed." Psalm 91 was in full effect against these unexpected cobra attacks. These sneaky cobra attacks are the things our military face on a daily basis, but God has a promise for us if we pray preventatively—we can miss danger that we never knew was coming.

Brian says: "Our entire company prayed Psalm 91 before, during, and after each mission. It became complete standard practice to see soldiers, regardless of nationality, religion, or gender, handwriting the entire Psalm 91, word for word, and then placing that covenant into their uniforms close to their heart. Sometimes you would see scriptures even attached to personal equipment. Prayers, prior to the end of and at the completion of combat operations, would be publicly spoken. Psalm 91 had even turned those who were once skeptics into full-fledged believers in God's protection. Each day soldiers would go out and pray over their vehicle, their equipment, and over each other. And each day the number of soldiers performing these public faith actions would increase."[1] We definitely need God's protection from cobra attacks.

The previous figurative examples we might have guessed, but what are the "dragon problems"? The Hebrew word for *dragon* translates to "sea monster."[2] First of all, there is no such thing as a dragon or a sea monster. Dragons are a figment of one's imagination. But have you ever experienced fears that were a figment of your imagination? Sure you have. We all have.

Dragon problems represent our unfounded fears, phantom fears, or mirage fears. That sounds harmless enough, but are you aware that phantom fears can be as deadly as reality fears if we believe them?

Some people's dragon fears are as real to them as another person's lion problems. That is why it is important to define your fears. So many people spend all of their lives running from something that is not even chasing them. Many people come home from combat, and what was once a lion problem becomes a phantom problem they battle the rest of their lives.

Proverbs 28:1 says, "The wicked flee when no one is pursuing," and is a good definition of phantom fears.

We have had a great many people share testimonies of
God's deliverance from things like fear of the unknown,
fear of facing the future alone, fear of loss, fear of death,
tormenting suspicions, or claustrophobia. Dragon fear
is a very valid form of spiritual attack—especially for
soldiers who have been subjected to extended periods of
intense battle. When my daughter and her husband lived
in an apartment when they first married, their manager
was a Vietnam veteran. Angelia came up behind him one
day to bring their rent check, and he went into "attack
mode." Afterward he apologized profusely, but his body
was still living in the past. He was out of danger, but
he was still dwelling there. Others experience mental
gymnastics and restless nights—rehearsing all the things
that can go wrong in each situation. Dragon fears keep
one living in the past or the future rather than experiencing life in the present. Fantasy fears can cause us to
do a lot of unnecessary running in life, so authority over
dragons is not a mental game.

But the good news is that God says we will tread
on all of the powers of the enemy, no matter how loud
and bold, sneaky and deceptive, or imaginary the fears
might be. God has given us authority over all of them!

No longer are we to put up with the paralyzing fears
that at one time gripped our hearts and left us powerless
at the sight of the evil that was striking all around us.
God has given us His power of attorney, and these problems now have to submit to the authority of His name.

I like that word *tread*. I think of a tank crossing a

brushy plain. Where the tank treads go, everything is crushed and left flat on the ground. It is a great picture of our authority over these spiritual enemies as well, treading like a tank and crushing all that is evil in our path. That is a strong description of our authority in walking over the lion, young lion, cobra, and dragon.

Chapter

BECAUSE I LOVE HIM

Because he has loved Me, therefore I
will deliver him.

—PSALM 91:14

IN VERSES 14–16 THE psalm moves from talking
in the third person about God's promises to God
speaking to us personally from His secret place and
announcing His promises Himself, in the first person.
It is a dramatic shift in tone as it moves to God speaking
prophetically to each one of us directly, denoting
significantly more depth in the relationship. In these
three verses He gives seven promises with as much
open triumph as a man has when a woman accepts his
proposal. Setting your love involves choice. When you
pick that person out of all the others, you set your love
on that one and you embark on a deeper relationship.
That is the picture of how God sets His love. Love is the
cohesiveness that binds man to God, and God will be
faithful to His beloved. Love always requires presence

86

and nearness. Special memories are birthed out of relationship. That is why this section cannot be explained but has to be experienced.

Many of us have watched in horror when a child picked up a newborn kitten by the throat and carried it all over the yard, and we wondered how the kitten ever survived. We had an old red hen that endured distress from our very enthusiastic children. Old Red allowed herself to be picked up while in the process of laying her egg and would deposit it right in Angie's eager little hands. The children had some merit to what they advertised as the freshest eggs in town; there were a few times when an egg never hit the nest.

Nesting season had its own special fascination for the children as they watched Old Red try to hatch out more eggs than she could sit on. The kids would number the eggs in pencil to ensure each egg was properly rotated and kept warm. They would wait out the twenty-one days and then, with contagious delight, call me out to see the nest swarming with little ones. That old hen had a brood of chicks that was hatched out of eggs from every hen in the henhouse.

Observing a setting hen this closely had its own rare charm as one could witness the protection she gave those chicks in a way most people never have the chance to observe. I remember her feathers as she fanned them out. I remember the smell of the fresh straw the kids kept in the nest. I remember that I could see through the soft, downy underside and see the rhythmic beating of her heart. Those chicks had an almost enviable position, something all the books on the theology of protection could never explain in mere words. This was the unforgettable picture of a real-life understanding of what it means to be under the wings. Those were some happy chicks! This lets one see in a much more intimate way that true protection has everything to do with closeness.

Some people acknowledge that there is a God; others *know* Him. Maturity, education, family heritage, or even living a lifetime as a nominal Christian cannot make a person *know* Him. Only an encounter with the Lord and time spent with Him will cause us to lay hold of the promises in these verses.

We need to ask ourselves, "Do I really love Him?" Jesus even asked this of Peter, who was a close disciple, "Simon [Peter]...do you love Me?" (John 21:15). Can you imagine how Peter must have felt when Jesus questioned him three times, "Simon [Peter]...do you love Me?" Even so, we need to question ourselves, because these promises are made only to those who have genuinely set their love on Him. Take special note of the fact that these seven promises are reserved for those who return His Love. Remember the Lord said in John 14:15, "If you love Me, you will keep My commandments." Our obedience is an extremely reliable telltale sign that shows us we really love Him. Do you love Him? If you do, these promises are for you.

Chapter

GOD IS MY DELIVERER

Because he has loved Me, therefore I
will deliver him.

—Psalm 91:14

A PROMISE OF DELIVERANCE IS the first of the seven promises made to the one who loves God. Make it personal! For instance, I quote it like this: "Because I love You, Lord, I thank You for Your promise to deliver me." There are several types of deliverances. There is the internal and the external. Ask yourself, "From what is He going to deliver me?" Remember the external deliverances discussed in previous chapters?

God will deliver us from all of the following:

- The lion problems
- The young lion problems
- The cobra problems
- The dragon problems

- The terror by night (evils that come through man: war, terror, or violence)
- The arrows that fly by day (enemy assignments sent to wound)
- The pestilence (plagues, deadly diseases, fatal epidemics)
- The destruction (evils over which man has no control)

In other words, God wants to deliver us from every evil known to mankind. That protection does not stop just because we might be on foreign soil, alone on a dangerous mission, or in the midst of a fierce battle.

Army Chaplain Captain Jesus M. Perez experienced God's deliverance shortly after he joined the army in 1998; he shares that experience here.

"I joined the army in 1998 and was sent to Korea. Still searching for my Jewish roots, it was there I met some Korean Jews, which was awesome. While playing football, I got tackled by two airmen, which fractured my back in three pieces. I was taken to the ER and told by the doctor, 'Corporal Perez, I regret to inform you that you will never walk again.' That was devastating, because my dream had always been to be a chaplain since I was eight years old. I stayed in the hospital, strapped in the bed, for about three weeks. They were trying to decide what to do with me because I was no good to the army now. The X-rays, MRIs, and medical procedures revealed that my L5 and S1 were completely shredded. I had no motion in my legs. When the doctor told me that I was not going to walk again, I asked him, 'Doctor, is this your professional opinion?' He said, 'Yes, it is.'

"So I said, 'I have news for you. God has something else to say about this. I am trusting God to get me out of this bed because I want to be a chaplain, and neither you, this fracture, or anybody else is going to stop me.' So that night was Sabbath, and I prayed, 'If You are the powerful God of the Jews, and I am a Jew, I am asking that You perform in me the same miracles that You did for the people of the Bible. I need You to raise me out of this bed, not because I need to see it, but because they need to believe it.' So that night I called the nurse and asked her to take off the straps and the catheter. She said, 'I will take it out, but don't do anything strange. I know you want to get out of this bed.' She left, and the man in the bed beside me said, 'What are you thinking?' I said, 'I just want to go to the bathroom.' So he said, 'You can't leave the bed. You will fall.' And I said, 'No, I won't.' So I got my legs off the side of the bed and started walking down the hall. He started hollering, 'He's walking. Look at him. He's walking.' The nurse came running, and when she saw me walking, she said, 'What are you doing?' When I came out of the bathroom, there was quite a commotion. Everyone was in an uproar.

"So they sent me to Japan to confirm that I did indeed have a fractured back. When the navy neurologist surgeon saw my X-rays and MRI, he asked me, 'Where is this soldier?' I said, 'I'm right here, sir,' and he said, 'No, don't play games with me because whoever these X-rays and MRIs belong to could not possibly walk! You are walking. So, I don't have time for games.' Then he said, 'If this is so, I will believe that God indeed has performed a miracle in your life.'

"Today I am living my dream of becoming a chaplain with two tours to Iraq and an awesome ministry as the first Messianic rabbi in the US Army."[1]

Each war has its testimonies of deliverance. Another fascinating story comes from Andrew Wommack during his deployment in Vietnam from January 1970 through the end of February 1971, where he served in the 196th Infantry Brigade as an assistant to the chaplain. He writes:

> I pulled bunker duty on landing zone (LZ) west; there was a bunker out on a finger of that 441-meter-tall hill. It was so steep that this hill was almost impregnable, except for one way you could come up, and that was where this bunker was located. It was sort of an outpost, and I was down there with three other guys pulling bunker guard. I pulled the first guard duty, and there was a guy who sat up on top with me. He was a Puerto Rican who had been drafted and didn't speak any English. I tried talking to him, and all he would say was, "Forty days." I asked, "Have you been in the country forty days?" He would simply say, "Forty days." I couldn't talk

to him, so I pulled my four-hour bunker guard, and then I lay on top of the bunker and went to sleep.

"We're supposed to stay there until six, but when I woke up about three or four in the morning, everyone was gone. I didn't know what had happened, so I finished up the bunker guard until six o'clock and then headed up the hill. The chaplain met me and asked if I was all right or if I had been hurt, and I said, "What are you talking about?" It turned out while I was sleeping right beside this Puerto Rican, he had gone crazy and shot off every M-16 round he had—hundreds of them.

"He threw probably 100 or 150 hand grenades. He shot a hundred or so M-69 grenade launchers, and he fired off four or five claymore mines. This guy was crazy, and the other guys who were pulling bunker guard with us got scared and ran up the hill while he was still shooting and throwing hand grenades. The people there were ready to blow him away because they didn't know what on earth he was doing; they knew he had a tremendous amount of ammunition down there, but they also knew I was still down there, so they couldn't do anything. The uncanny part is that I slept through the whole thing while this guy just went totally crazy, but God protected me through the whole ordeal. "Because he [Andrew Wommack] has loved Me, therefore I will deliver him" (Ps. 91:14).[2]

Deliverance is all encompassing. It happens internally and externally; in fact, it surrounds us:

> You are my hiding place; You preserve me from trouble; You surround me with songs of deliverance. Selah.
>
> —Psalm 32:7

Chapter

I AM SEATED ON HIGH

> Because he has loved Me...I will set
> him securely on high, because he has
> known My name.
> —PSALM 91:14

To be set securely on high is the second promise to those who love the Lord and know Him by name. "It is My name," God says, "that has been on his lips when he faces troubles, and he has run to Me. He has called out to Me in faith; therefore, I will set him on high" (Ps. 91:14–15, author's paraphrase).

…which He brought about in Christ, when He raised Him from the dead and seated Him at His right hand in the heavenly places, far above all rule and authority and power and dominion, and every name that is named, not only in this age but also in the one to come.…and raised us up with Him,

and seated us with Him in the heavenly places in
Christ Jesus.

—EPHESIANS 1:20–21; 2:6

It is interesting that God pulls us up to where He is.
Things look better from higher up. Our vantage point is
much improved when we are seated with Him on high.

"Seated on high" took on a whole new meaning for
Jimmy Stewart when he joined the US Air Force in 1941,
even before the emotional Pearl Harbor attack made
most men angry enough to sign up. By that time he
had already moved from private to captain in the 445th
Bomb Group and was flying the B-24 bomber missions
deep into the heart of Nazi Germany and serving as
an instructor to train others. Stationed at the base in
Tibenham, England, Stewart was given the assign-
ment of training men to enter the war to fly missions
to destroy as many of the German Luftwaffe fighter
planes as possible. Two of his training crews were killed
before they even entered combat, and, to add insult to
injury, sixty men were lost in the first twenty-one days
of combat. Stewart had lost close friends and a number
of students. Life came close to being a nightmare.

Stewart told his men that they were going to fly
a Christmas Eve mission to hit the German's secret
rocket hideout in Bonnieres, France. Thirty-five planes
would be taken, and they would fly at an altitude of
twelve thousand in order to hit the necessary targets—
an announcement that brought stunned shock to his

men because that was so low. In his peaceful manner he simply told his men that the Germans had a new kind of rocket machine that they were planning to use to blow up many of the large cities in London. His calm response was simply: "We are going to have to see that they don't get that chance. I'm looking for volunteers." No one would be forced, but he qualified it with, "You can count on the fact I'm going."

There are no words to describe the weight that Captain Stewart carried on his shoulders as he planned that mission. More than ever Jimmy was depending on the gift of a promise his father had given him just as he was leaving the States. His father had handed him a note and asked him to read it sometime before his plane reached Europe, but Jimmy had the letter opened by the time the plane had barely cleared the runway.

My dear Jim boy,

Soon after you read this letter you will be on your way to the worst sort of danger. I have had this in mind for a long time, and I am very much concerned... But Jim, I am banking on the enclosed copy of the 91st Psalm. The thing that takes the place of fear and worry is the promise in these words. I feel sure that God will lead you through this mad experience... I can say no more. I continue only to pray. Good-bye, my dear son. God bless and keep you. I love you more than I can tell you.

—Dad

Jimmy was never without that letter tucked in the pocket of his flight suit. According to plan, Stewart and his men spent Christmas Eve attacking the German secret weapon locations in France. He and his air patrol group returned to Tibenham *without losing a single plane*. Stewart also had in his pocket the book with the Psalms, Proverbs, and New Testament given to him when he enlisted. His book included a letter from President Franklin D. Roosevelt: "As Commander-in-Chief, I take pleasure in commending the reading of the Bible to all who serve in the armed forces of the United States. Throughout the centuries, men of many faiths and diverse origins have found in the Sacred Book words of wisdom, counsel, and inspiration. It is a fountain of strength, and now, as always, an aid in attaining the highest aspiration of the human soul."

When the US bombers came up against the German Luftwaffe, it was certainly no picnic. Every flier knew he was on a life-and-death mission. There are no words to describe the horrors of thirty combat missions, but Captain Stewart had the revered reputation of always bringing his squadron home safely. His dependence on Psalm 91 kept Stewart going. What he said about that psalm has often been quoted: "What a promise for an airman! I placed in His hands the squadron I would be leading. And, as the psalmist promised, I felt myself borne up." In 1959 Stewart earned the rank of brigadier general. Interesting, few people were aware that Stewart continued flying combat missions in Vietnam.

Back in Hollywood after the war, Jimmy Stewart filmed one of the movies for which he is best known: *It's a Wonderful Life*. But he never quit carrying his father's letter with him. That advice from Psalm 91 was of utmost importance to him—not just in wartime but up until his death on July 7, 1997. Psalm 91:11 was even engraved on his tombstone: "For He shall give his angels charge over thee to keep thee in all thy ways."

That was not the only promise in Psalm 91 that was exemplified in his life. The promises to protect him from terror (what man could do to harm him), from arrows (bullets), from pestilence (disease) and destruction (natural disasters), and the promises to deliver him, keep him from harm, rescue him from trouble, honor him, and satisfy him with a long life were all demonstrated in his life.[1]

It is so important to realize that the name you call on can save you. It can set you securely on high. Or you can use the name and speak evil, which gives no help to your situation. It makes no sense to have access to the name that can work miracles and deliver your life and not use it in a way that renders you mercy. Many times we lose spiritual battles with our mouths, and we open ourselves up for assaults. An environment of cursing opens the door for being cursed, yet calling on God for help renders aid. When you get a revelation of the power of that name, it not only causes you to refrain from evil, but it also gives you a reverence for Him, just as you would respect the name of one of your closest friends. I challenge you to meditate on God's promise: "I will set him on high because he has known My name." These are not just empty words.

In the first two sentences alone of Psalm 91, the psalmist refers to God by four different names, progressively denoting stronger relationship. The writer refers to God as the *Most High*, revealing that He is the highest thing that exists. This implies so much more significance when we realize we are set securely on high with the One who is Most High.

From on high we have a better vantage point and better perspective. In this opening of Psalm 91, God is also called the *Almighty*, denoting that He is "all" mighty—the most powerful. Next He is referred to as the *Lord*, revealing ownership. Then the psalmist calls Him *my God*, making it personal. We see God unveiled in four unique ways to the man who has known His name.

Verse 14 introduces two conditions and two promises that link back to the beginning of the psalm—"because he has loved Me" and "because he has known My name"—each introduced with the word *because* to catch our attention. Then He responds with two promises of deliverance and positioning. We love the fact that God faithfully keeps His promises, but have we kept ours?

A number of Iowa's 113th Cavalry, an outfit that fought superbly in the European war, received Easter cards that opened their eyes. The front of the card included a sketch of a German battlefield labeled Easter

1945. On top was the word *Remember*? in large letters. On the inside of the card was a family fireside sketch and the following: "Well, God did what you asked! He delivered you safely home and set you back on high. Now! Have you done what you promised? How about Easter 1950?" The card was signed by the Reverend Ben L. Rose, the pastor of the Central Presbyterian Church in Bristol, Virginia. This pastor should know their promises—he was the chaplain of the 113th Cavalry.[2]

Many times in dangerous situations we make God promises—foxhole commitments! What a reminder! Do I sincerely love Him? This chaplain wanted to make sure his men remembered their vows. Do I really know Him by name and trust in His promises? Have I been faithful to keep the promises I've made to Him?

Chapter

GOD ANSWERS MY CALL

> He will call upon Me, and I will
> answer him.
>
> —Psalm 91:15

GOD MAKES A THIRD promise here in verse 15 that He will answer those who truly love Him and call on His name. Are we aware of what a wonderful promise God is making to us here?

> This is the confidence which we have before Him, that, if we ask anything according to His will, He hears us. And if we know that He hears us in whatever we ask, we know that we have the requests which we have asked from Him.
>
> —1 John 5:14–15

Nothing gives me more comfort than to realize that every time I pray in line with God's Word, He hears me. If He hears me, I know I have the request for which I

asked. This one promise keeps me continually searching
His Word in order to understand His will and His
promises so I can know how to pray more effectively.
Sometimes I just cry out to God for help. Soon after
Andrew Gray returned from his second tour of duty in
Afghanistan, a long, fifteen-month tour, he celebrated
his return with a trip to New York for his fiancée's
birthday. His mother tells the story of God's answer to
his call for help during his visit to New York. "We were
to pick him up at the airport the evening of January 15.
It had been a sweet, sweet time for Stephanie and him,
and his dad and I were looking forward to his coming
home and spending time with us.

"The phone rang, and it was Andrew calling. He
started the conversation with, 'I'm all right.' My
husband's immediate thought was, 'Well, of course you
are.' Then Andrew proceeded to tell his dad that his plane
just went down in the Hudson River and to turn on the
TV. That was all he had time to tell us. His dad and I
rushed to turn on the TV. There was breaking news of
Flight 1549 crashing into the Hudson River. We stared
incredulously at the screen as we saw the footage of this
airplane just floating in the water. The right wing was
listing. We watched and waited to hear from him again.

"When he called again, he told us he and Stephanie
had been on the right wing of the plane, which had been
sinking. They had stepped out in frigid water up to their
ankles, and it wasn't long before the water was rising up
above their knees. They were being pushed farther and

farther to the tip of the wing as more passengers came out of the emergency door.

"As Andrew recalled the events of the day, he said he knew there was something wrong with the airplane when he heard a loud pop and then saw black smoke coming from the engine. As the plane banked to make a turn, Andrew reassured Stephanie that it would be all right; they weren't far out from the airport, and the plane was returning to land. As they looked out the window, Andrew realized there was a strange silence on the airplane. Usually you can hear the hum of the engines, but he couldn't hear any engine at all. At that time he knew they were only gliding. Losing altitude quickly, he knew they were in trouble. When the pilot came over the intercom and told them to brace for impact, Stephanie was crying, and Andrew knew they would be going down in the water. He said he was somewhat relieved that they would be going into the water rather than hitting land. He thought that might give them more of a chance for survival. He said he had a spark of hope, mingled with fear. He was telling Stephanie that if they somehow survived the crash, that they would need to get off of the plane in a hurry. They kissed each other, said 'I love you,' huddled close to one another, and started praying together, bracing for the impact."

Andrew and his brother had served missions in Iraq and Afghanistan without serious injury, due, in no small part, to their mother. Mary Gray had discovered Psalm 91 and taken it to heart. She had prayed the psalm over her sons every single day. She'd gotten a whole group of people to pray for them as well. She had told her sons to pray Psalm 91, and she gave each of them a camouflage bandana with Psalm 91 printed on it to remind them to do just that.

In 2006 she began a ministry called Operation Bandanas, sending out Psalm 91 bandanas to other sons and daughters as a ministry of spiritual support and encouragement to those serving our country. Perfect for protecting the face during a windstorm, the bandanas also protected the head from blistering sun. But that wasn't their only protection; each bandana had been imprinted with Psalm 91. To date, this mother has provided more than 160,000 men and women in the US military serving overseas in harm's way.

Andrew remembered the way men in his brigade had read the Psalm. Even those who weren't religious found comfort in the words. During two tours, he was proud that the men under his command escaped Afghanistan with no loss of life, limb, or eyesight. He believed that Psalm 91 was more than a myth passed from one generation of soldiers to another. It was more than a legend. He believed it was a powerful promise to anyone who would believe it—and he and Stephanie were depending on that promise as they sat in the airplane at that very moment.

Andrew's mom continued, "By the grace of God and with the experience of a very skilled pilot, the airplane did a relatively smooth landing on the water. They unbuckled their seat belts quickly, and Andrew guided Stephanie down the aisle to the emergency door on the wing. The pilot, Captain Sullenberger, was at the terminal where Andrew was taken. He seemed calm, drinking a cup of coffee, with one of his hands in his pocket. I'm sure, though, that he also was in a state of shock. There was much celebration and thanks being given to him from everyone at the terminal. God had certainly used him that day."[1]

God protects us!

As important as individual praying is, nothing seems to compare to a nation praying in faith. When English soldiers were trapped at Dunkirk—with the German army behind them and the English Channel in front of them—the prime minister warned the nation that no more than twenty or thirty thousand of the two hundred thousand British soldiers could possibly be rescued from those exposed beaches. But no one could have estimated the power of a nation in prayer. The churches of England were filled—the king and queen knelt at Westminster Abby, the Archbishop of Canterbury, the prime minister, the cabinet, and all of Parliament were on their knees.[2]

Suddenly, one of the Nazi generals decided to regroup and ordered a halt of the German troops when they were only twelve miles away from Dunkirk, and Hitler made a rash decision to hold them there indefinitely. The weather suddenly proved to be a great hindrance to the enemy planes firing on the English troops who appeared to be trapped like mice on that French coast. Instantly, every imaginable vessel that would float—everything from private boats piloted by bank clerks, fishermen, Boy Scouts, yachtsmen, barge operators, college professors, and tugboat captains started their rescue mission. Even London fire brigade boats got in on the action. Shipyards were quickly set up to repair the damaged vessels so they could return for another load. Anyone would have said the undertaking was absurd, but the prayers of a nation strengthened them in one of the most dangerous and seemingly impossible endeavors in all history.

On the boats taking them to safety, the men began to pray—many of whom had never prayed before. At the camps in England the men requested permission to pray. It became apparent to all of Britain that their prayers were being heard. More than 7,000 troops were evacuated the first day. In the final total there were 338,000 British, Belgian, and French troops brought to safety.[3]

Collective prayers were being called for on both sides of the ocean at strategic turning points of the war. President Franklin Roosevelt from America issued a proclamation for prayer, and a nation responded.[4]

What tremendous testimonies to the might of the combined prayers of the masses! When we think of the power of individual prayer, let's not forget history's record of what happens by the power of corporate prayer—when a nation prays, when a city prays, when leaders pray...it strengthens the individual's prayer. When soldiers call upon God—He answers. When nations call upon God—history records it.

Chapter

GOD RESCUES ME
FROM TROUBLE

I will be with him in trouble; I will
rescue him.

—Psalm 91:15

THE FOURTH PROMISE, TO rescue from trouble
those who love the Lord, is found in the middle
of verse 15. It is a well-known fact that human
nature cries out to God when faced with trouble. Men
in prison, soldiers in war, people in accidents all seem to
call out to God when they get in a crisis. Even atheists
are known to call on the God they don't acknowledge
when they are extremely afraid. A lot of criticism has
been given to those last-resort prayers. However, in
defense of this kind of praying, we must remember
when one is in pain, he usually runs to the one he loves
the most and the one he trusts. The alternative is not

calling out at all, so this verse acknowledges calling out to God in trouble is a good place for a person to start!

God answers our prayers and rescues us in so many different ways. I am so thankful He is creative and not hindered by our seemingly impossible situations. But we have to ask in faith and not confine Him to our limited resources. God says, "If you love Me, I will be with you when you find yourself in trouble, and I will rescue you." But we have to trust Him to do it His way.

> When you pass through the waters, I will be with you; and through the rivers, they will not overflow you. When you walk through the fire, you will not be scorched, nor will the flame burn you.
>
> —Isaiah 43:2

During the years of World War II, the pastor and congregation of a church in Dallas, Texas, prayed continually for the men who had deployed, praying at the altar over them for the protection of Psalm 91 and other protection verses over the men until they returned home safely. That was Spencer January's home church, and Spencer, who served in the Army's 35th Infantry, went to that altar for prayer before he deployed. That protection was powerfully impacting to him.

In 1945 his division had just been ordered to take the town of Ossenburg, Germany, where a war factory supplied Hitler's troops. Forcing his way through the dense German forest, Spencer was plagued with the thought that they might never make it back home alive.

His group had been fighting for hours to get through the thick jungle-like terrain when suddenly they came to an open space with a large stone house. They were aware that the large stone house in the opening was concealing a handful of wounded, bleeding soldiers who had tried earlier to cross the clearing and failed. Soon three nests of German machine guns suddenly began blasting away, but they were still too far out of range for the barrage of bullets to take Spencer and his fellow soldiers out.

It was sure death to cross the opening, but it was the 35th Infantry's only avenue since every other passage into town was secured by the Germans. The team was in a quandary. They knew there was no way to live to tell the tale if they tried to push on through the clearing. It was impossible for Spencer not to think of his wife and five-month-old son he had left back home. The odds were a thousand to one that he had seen them for the last time. Pain surged through his entire being with that thought. His only hope was a miracle from God. Time was running out, and at any moment his group would be running right though the barrage of open fire. Before he even knew what he was doing, he found himself on his knees, praying passionately, "God, You've got to help me! *Please*, do something!"

Spencer barely had time to finish his desperate prayer when the group was ordered to advance. Memories of home and family crashed down on him as he gripped his rifle and made his way across the clearing to the other edge of the forest covering. The painful thought that he would probably never see his family again stayed with him every step of the way.

Suddenly a huge white cloud materialized in what had been, only moments before, a totally clear sky. The cloud dropped down and shrouded the clearing, almost like an eclipse. There was no way for the Germans to see where to fire. Instantly Spencer and his fellow soldiers took off like runners in a race—this time competing not for a medal but for their very lives.

Almost beyond belief, Spencer found himself across the clearing and into the thicket. Many more of his group were making it across. The ones in the very back were having to pull some of the wounded to safety, but even those were making it. No one had to tell him that what he had just experienced was God. As quickly as the miracle cloud had appeared, just as the last soldier made it across, the cloud vanished miraculously. Then suddenly, the earth literally shook in convulsions as the Germans launched a bomb that blew the stone house into tiny pieces. It became obvious that they did not realize Spencer and his group had already crossed the clearing in obscurity.

All the way to Ossenburg Spencer kept thinking about that cloud. He was accustomed to the smoke screens that were used to hide the troops, but this was entirely different. This was not a man-made covering. He and the other men knew it was a supernatural intervention. And to continue His miracle, God helped them overtake the war factory in Ossenburg.

A short time later, Spencer received a letter from his mother that had finally caught up with him. The words in the letter sent a shiver down his spine as he realized how God had spared the men. His mother told him that Mrs. Tankersly, a woman from the church who prayed faithfully for the soldiers, had called to tell her about a spiritual visitation from God on the very night when the men were actually facing the enemy fire in that clearing. God told her, "Spencer January is in trouble! Get up right now and pray for him!" Mrs. Tankersly said that she had prayed until time to go to work, and the last thing she remembered praying was: "Lord, whatever danger Spencer is in, just cover him with a cloud!" She told Spencer's mother that she had finished praying at 6:00 a.m.

By the time he finished reading, Spencer was shaking so hard that he could barely see to read the letter. He realized there was a seven-hour difference in time, so Mrs. Tankersly had been praying just as his group came upon the German ambush. Her prayer for God to send a cloud covering would have been prayed at one o'clock in the afternoon in Germany—just when they were ready to dash across the danger zone.

God's supernatural protection made such an impression on Spencer that he dedicated the early morning hours every day for the next sixty years to pray for friends and relatives. After the miracle intervention in Germany, no one could have taken away his faith in the difference that prayer can make. He was convinced beyond a shadow of a doubt that the prayer of that one faithful woman back in 1945 had saved not only his life but also the lives of the other soldiers with him as they ran unseen through the cloud covering.

After his time of serving in World War II, he continued on as a soldier, but this time as a faithful soldier in the Lord's army. There is no way to know all the miracles that followed the wake of those fervent prayers that Spencer January prayed.

Although some people might call happenings like these a coincidence, the negative situations that we encounter can become God-incidences when we trust His Word.[1]

Chapter

GOD HONORS ME

[I will] honor him.

—PSALM 91:15

THE FIFTH PROMISE, TO honor those who love God, is in the last part of verse 15. All of us like to be honored. I can remember the teacher calling my name when I was in grade school and complimenting a paper I had turned in. That thrilled me. I was honored.

Several years ago our daughter, Angelia, attended a political rally in our city that was given for George W. Bush when he was campaigning for Texas governor. She had shared a quick personal anecdote with him at the beginning of the meeting when they first met. After he had spoken to the group and was leaving with some of his colleagues, everyone was shocked when he left his group and darted back to our daughter to say, "Remember the promise I made; no tears for you in November." She was honored that he had taken her amusing story as a personal challenge and left a very demanding crowd to seal the deal.

When this book was written, our granddaughter's husband, Heath Adams, was a staff sergeant in the US Air Force. He had recently finished Airman Leadership School and was then stationed at Great Falls, Montana. We were all thrilled when he received the John Levitow Award, the highest award given at the leadership school banquet. It was not only an honor for him, but it was also an honor for his whole squadron. Then he was one of eight people chosen from forty-five hundred security forces to represent Air Force Space Command in the Defender Challenge Competition, where his team took silver medals in the obstacle course and tactics events, placing second overall.

Heath was also a distinguished graduate at Security Force Level II Combat Leaders Course. He won the Air Force SF Noncommissioned Officer Award at 20th Air Force and had the honor of giving a warrior brief to the secretary of the air force—the first warrior brief the secretary had ever heard. The commander coordinated a surprise ceremony to give Heath his promotion and secretly arranged for our granddaughter, Jolena, to be there. Not only was his military service noted, but also his character as a family man, a youth pastor, and, ultimately, a faithful follower of Christ, evidenced in his activity with a local church, was communicated to the group. The ceremony honored Heath before all his peers.

Men have many types of customs to honor other men,

from ceremonies and speeches to medals of distinction. I have had the highest admiration for each serviceman I have interviewed as they showed me their Purple Hearts and their medals of honor. Those are symbols of the honors that have been bestowed on those recipients.

Not only is it an honor, but it also feels good to have someone we consider important pay special attention to us. It is a thrill to be honored by man, *but how much more of a tribute and a thrill when we are honored by God!* Fulfilling our part of the covenant allows God to honor us.

Have you ever thought about what it means to be honored by the God of the universe? He honors us by calling us His sons and daughters. He honors us by answering when we take His Word seriously and call out to Him in faith. He honors us by recognizing us individually and by preparing a place for us to be with Him eternally. Giving us honor is one of the seven unique bonus promises made in Psalm 91.

Chapter

GOD SATISFIES ME
WITH LONG LIFE

With a long life I will satisfy him.
—PSALM 91:16

THE SIXTH PROMISE, TO satisfy those who love Him with a long life, is found in verse 16. God does not only say He will prolong our lives and give us a lot of birthdays. No! He says He will satisfy us with a long life. There are people who would testify that simply having a great many birthdays is not necessarily a blessing. But God says He will give us many birthdays, and as those birthdays roll around we will experience satisfaction. It has been said there is a God-shaped vacuum on the inside of each one of us. Man has tried to fill that vacuum with many different things, but nothing will satisfy the emptiness until it is filled with Jesus. He is the true satisfaction to which God refers in His promise.

God is making the offer. If we will come to Him, let Him fill that empty place on the inside, and allow Him to fulfill the call on our lives, then He will give us a long life and satisfy us as we live it out. Only the dissatisfied person can really appreciate what it means to find satisfaction.

But let's not neglect the promise of a long life. King David was Israel's most valiant, daring warrior, yet he lived to a ripe old age, full of days as the Old Testament liked to say. His life was filled with combat, high-risk situations, and impossible odds. Yet he did not die in battle, but his head went down in peace in his old age. Long life is a great concluding promise of protection.

Paul lets us know in Ephesians that we are in a fight. We can't flow with what feels good and win this battle because the enemy will make the wrong path extremely easy to take. Once, in a boat on the Sea of Galilee, the disciples cried out, fearing they would drown in the storm. However, Jesus had said they must go to the other side. If they had thought through what He had said, they would have known the storm would not harm them because they had His word concerning a mission across the lake. In the same way, if you have been promised a satisfying long life, then you know you will make it through the present circumstances.

Colonel James E. Agnew made it through many dangerous situations during his military career, including the following, which took place during Desert Storm. He tells the story.

"While I served as the First Cavalry Division Support Command Chaplain during Operation Desert Storm, my troop coverage responsibility included the Division Chemical Platoon. Finding enemy chemical warfare strategy would not have come as a surprise. Most of the world was still in shock over the brutality of Saddam Hussein's attacks. The United Nations Security Council had threatened to use force if he didn't withdraw from Kuwait, but instead, he began advancing toward Saudi Arabia and fired the first seven Scud missiles at Israel. In anticipation of what was coming, the United States had begun shipping in more than three hundred thousand troops.

"Since Hussein had promised to use chemical warfare against any opposition, naturally, the first to go into battle would be the Platoon's Chemical Division to determine if, in fact, there was chemical warfare, and if so, what type was there and how much. No one doubted Hussein's threats after the horrible things he had done to his own people.

"Prior to the beginning of the ground war, my mission included visiting all the troopers preparing to move forward. Being first on the battle field presented numerous challenges for these men with an increased risk of contact, ambush, minefields, and chemical contamination. These soldiers were well aware of the risks and skillfully trained to deal with whatever obstacle they might encounter, but fear was ever present.

"I was making the last leg of my journey on foot.

We had traveled over dangerous territory to reach this frontline unit, but I wanted to visit and pray with this Chemical Platoon group of men before they crossed the border into Kuwait. It was an early morning visit, and I noticed they had already gathered into a circle around the platoon leader. I thought to myself, 'This is great; I'll have a captive audience of the entire platoon already waiting for me.'

"As I got closer, I noticed they had Bibles in their hands and were about to have their daily devotional as a platoon. They were thrilled to see me and asked if I would read the Ninety-First Psalm and pray for them. Apparently they had started the morning formations by reading the Ninety-First Psalm and prayer ever since they arrived in Saudi. As the alert to move out had been given that day, the soldiers felt that the Lord had sent me at just the right time to speak peace to their hearts and encourage their faith just before they embarked on the most dangerous mission they had ever faced.

"As I began to read Psalm 91, I sensed the strong presence of the Lord among us. The anxious looks on the troopers' faces gave way to a calm, peaceful platoon to complete its mission with an unwavering faith that God was with them and that the promises of Psalm 91 were personally for them.

"At three o'clock the next morning those men crossed the border into Kuwait. The wind whistled across the desert in such vicious force, it could sandblast the hide off a man's face. I was concerned that the weather was not cooperating; however, suddenly the wind changed direction. I realized that if Hussein tried to use chemical weapons now, the wind would blow it right back on him and his troops!

God was certainly with us. The Chemical Platoon accomplished its mission *without a single casualty*. I knew in my heart that the Lord directed me to this 'divine appointment' that brought His presence and peace to some anxious troopers, enabling them to walk by faith and serve God and country with great success."[1]

God wants us to claim the promise of long life, but He also wants us to use our long life to live for Him. Ask yourself, "What am I going to do with my long life?"

Chapter

I BEHOLD HIS SALVATION

And let him see [behold] My salvation.
—PSALM 91:16

ALLOWING THOSE WHO LOVE Him to behold His salvation is the seventh promise found in the last part of verse 16. *Behold* simply means to see something and take hold of it and make it our own. God wants us to take hold of His salvation.

The movement of this last line in Psalm 91 triumphs our ultimate, final victory. The order of this sentence gives promise we will see salvation face-to-face during and after our long, satisfied life. This moves us beyond an intellectual knowledge of salvation to relationship. It secures our future, but it starts now. The Bible constantly reminds us, "Salvation is now! Today it has come!" Many people are surprised when they look up the word *salvation* in a Bible concordance and find it has a much deeper meaning than just a ticket to heaven. We often miss the richness of this promise.

According to *Strong's Concordance*, the word *salvation* includes health, healing, rescue, deliverance, safety, protection, and provision.[1] What more could we ask? God promises He will allow us to see and take hold of His health, His healing, His deliverance, His protection, and His provision.

Many people read Psalm 91 and simply see it with their eyes, but very few behold it in their lives. My prayer is for that to change. One of my biggest thrills after teaching this truth of God is having different people write or call, describing the ecstatic joy of having it come alive in their hearts. I love to hear the extent to which they have actually taken hold of this covenant and started experiencing it as a vital part of their existence.

You can be in the midst of a forsaken land with the enemy all around you, and you can still behold the salvation of the Lord. Many have actually experienced the sensation of the presence of the Lord in the midst of chaos. The truth about God's salvation, His protection, deliverance, health, and provision, is more than just wishful thinking. It is a promise of which one can actually take hold.

PERSONAL PSALM
91 COVENANT

Copy and enlarge this Psalm 91 covenant prayer to pray over yourself and your loved ones, inserting his or her name in the blanks:

_____ dwells in the shelter of the Most High and he/she abides in the shadow of the Almighty. _____ says to the Lord, "My refuge and my fortress, my God, in whom I trust!" For it is God who delivers _____ from the snare of the trapper and from the deadly pestilence [fatal, infectious disease]. God will cover _____ with His pinions, and under His wings _____ may seek refuge; God's faithfulness is a shield and bulwark. _____ will not be afraid of the terror by night, or of the arrow that flies by day; of the pestilence that stalks in darkness, or of the destruction that lays waste at noon. One thousand may fall at _____ side, and ten thousand at his/her right hand; but it shall not approach _____. _____ will only look on with _____ eyes, and see the recompense of the wicked. For _____ has made the Lord, his/her refuge, even the Most High, _____'s dwelling place. No evil will befall _____, nor will any plague come near _____'s tent. For He will give His angels charge concerning _____ to guard _____ in all his/her ways. They will bear _____ up in their hands, lest _____ strike his/her foot against a stone. _____ will tread upon the lion and cobra, the young lion and the serpent he/she will trample down. "Because _____ has loved Me," [God said], "therefore I will deliver him/her; I will set _____ securely on high, because _____ has known My name. _____ will call on Me, and I will answer _____. I will be with _____ in trouble; I will rescue _____ and honor _____. With a long life I will satisfy _____, and let him/her behold My salvation.

"WHAT MUST I DO TO BE SAVED?"

W E HAVE TALKED ABOUT physical protection. Now let's make sure you have eternal security. The promises from God in this book are for God's children who love Him. If you have never given your life to Jesus and accepted Him as your Lord and Savior, there is no better time than right now.

There is none righteous, not even one.
—ROMANS 3:10

For all have sinned and fall short of the glory of God.
—ROMANS 3:23

But God demonstrates His own love toward us, in that while we were yet sinners, Christ died for us.
—ROMANS 5:8

For God so loved the world [you], that He gave His only begotten Son, that whoever believes in Him shall not perish, but have eternal life.
—JOHN 3:16

There is nothing we can do to earn our salvation or to make ourselves good enough to go to heaven. It is a free gift!

For the wages of sin is death, but the free gift of
God is eternal life in Christ Jesus our Lord.
—Romans 6:23

There is also no other avenue through which we can
reach heaven, other than Jesus Christ, God's Son.

And there is salvation in no one else; for there is
no other name under heaven that has been given
among men by which we must be saved.
—Acts 4:12

Jesus said to him, "I am the way, and the truth, and
the life; no one comes to the Father but through Me."
—John 14:6

You must believe that Jesus is the Son of God, that
He died on the cross for your sins, and that He rose
again on the third day.

Who [Jesus] was declared the Son of God with
power by the resurrection from the dead.
—Romans 1:4

You may be asking, "How do I accept Jesus and
become His child?" God in His love has made it so easy:

If you confess with your mouth Jesus as Lord, and believe in your heart that God raised Him from the dead, you will be saved.

—Romans 10:9

But as many as received Him, to them He gave the right to become children of God, even to those who believe in His name.

—John 1:12

It is as simple as praying a prayer similar to this one, if you sincerely mean it in your heart:

> *Dear God:*
>
> *I believe You gave Your Son, Jesus, to die for me. I believe He shed His blood to pay for my sins and that You raised Him from the dead so I can be Your child and live with You eternally in heaven. I am asking Jesus to come into my heart right now and save me. I confess Him as the Lord and Master of my life.*
>
> *I thank You, dear Lord, for loving me enough to lay down Your life for me. Take my life now and use it for Your glory. I ask for all that You have for me.*
>
> *In Jesus's name, amen.*

NOTES

Foreword

1. H. A. deWeerd, ed., *Selected Speeches and Statements of General of the Army George C. Marshall* (Washington DC: The Infantry Journal, 1945), quoted in Carl Joachim Hambro, "The Nobel Peace Prize 1953 Presentation Speech," December 10, 1953, http://www.nobelprize.org/nobel_prizes/peace/laureates/1953/press.html (accessed November 22, 2011).

Introduction

1. Walter B. Knight, *Knight's Master Book of 4,000 Illustrations* (Grand Rapids, MI: William B. Eerdman's Publishing Company, 1981), 526.

Chapter 1—Where Is My Dwelling Place?

1. Carey H. Cash, *A Table in the Presence* (Nashville, TN: Thomas Nelson, 2004), 217.

2. Excerpted from Peggy Joyce Ruth and Angelia Ruth Schum, *Psalm 91* (Lake Mary, FL: Charisma House, 2010), 220–221.

3. Katherine Pollard Carter, *The Mighty Hand of God* (Kirkwood, MO: Impact Christian Books, 1992), 34–35.

Chapter 2—What Is Coming Out of My Mouth?

1. Excerpted from Ruth and Schum, *Psalm 91*, 234–237.

2. Carter, *The Mighty Hand of God*, 29–30.

Chapter 3—Two-Way Deliverance

1. Excerpted from Ruth and Schum, *Psalm 91*, 212–214.

Chapter 4—Under His Wings

1. Excerpted from Ruth and Schum, *Psalm 91*, 239–241.

Chapter 5—A Mighty Fortress Is My God

1. Herbert Lockyer, ed., *Nelson's Illustrated Bible Dictionary* (Nashville, TN: Thomas Nelson, Inc., 1995), s.v. "bulwark."
2. Joseph H. Friend and David B. Guralnik, eds., *Webster's New World Dictionary* (New York: The World Publishing Co., 1953), s.v. "bulwark."
3. Carter, *The Mighty Hand of God*, 31–32.
4. Ibid., 29–30.

Chapter 6—I Will Not Fear the Terror

1. Carter, *The Mighty Hand of God*, 128–132.

Chapter 7—I Will Not Fear the Arrow

1. Excerpted from Peggy Joyce Ruth, *Psalm 91: God's Shield of Protection* (Lake Mary, FL: Creation House, 2007), 125–126.

Chapter 8—*I Will Not Fear the Pestilence*

1. James Strong, *Strong's Exhaustive Concordance of the Bible* (Madison, NJ: Abingdon Press, 1974), s.v. "*pino*."

2. Friend and Guralnik, *Webster's New World College Dictionary*, s.v. "imbibe."

3. Excerpted from Ruth and Schum, *Psalm 91*, 177–181.

Chapter 9—*I Will Not Fear the Destruction*

1. Excerpted from Ruth, *Psalm 91: God's Shield of Protection*, 153–157.

Chapter 10—*Though a Thousand Fall*

1. Excerpted from Ruth, *Psalm 91: God's Shield of Protection*, 187–193.

Chapter 11—*No Plague Comes Near My Family*

1. Excerpted from Ruth and Schum, *Psalm 91*, 194–198.

Chapter 12—*Angels Watching Over Me*

1. Alan S. Coulson and Michael E. Hanlon, "The Case of the Elusive Angel of Mons," Legends and Traditions of the Great War, http://www.worldwar1.com/heritage/angel.htm (accessed November 23, 2011).

2. Excerpted from Ruth, *Psalm 91: God's Shield of Protection*, 204–205.

Chapter 13—The Enemy Under My Feet

1. Brian Spears—National Guard, Georgia's 48th Brigade with Delta Company, 2nd Platoon, 1st Battalion, 121st Infantry—sent his testimony to the author via personal e-mail.

2. Strong, *Strong's Exhaustive Concordance of the Bible*, s.v. "dragon."

Chapter 15—God Is My Deliverer

1. Excerpted from Ruth, *Psalm 91: God's Shield of Protection*, 8th printing, 2009, 216–217.

2. Excerpted from Ruth and Schum, *Psalm 91*, 221–222.

Chapter 16—I Am Seated on High

1. This story about Jimmy Stewart can be found in the book by Starr Smith, *Jimmy Stewart Bomber Pilot* (Minneapolis, MN: Zenith Press, 2006). Also, "Jimmy Stewart in World War II," http://jodavidsmeyer.com/combat/military/jimmy_stewart.html (accessed November 28, 2011).

2. Knight, *Knight's Master Book of 4,000 Illustrations*, 531.

Chapter 17—God Answers My Call

1. Excerpted from Ruth and Schum, *Psalm 91*, 147–149.

2. Carter, *The Mighty Hand of God*, 29–30.

3. Joe Kissell, "The Battle of Dunkirk," *Interesting Thing of the Day*, http://itotd.com/articles/436/the-battle-of-dunkirk (accessed November 28, 2011).

4. FDR Library, "Franklin Roosevelt's D-Day Prayer," *Our Documents: D-Day*, http://docs.fdrlibrary.marist.edu/odddayp.html (accessed November 28, 2011).

Chapter 18—God Rescues Me From Trouble

1. Author's personal interview with Kay McCrary, daughter of Spencer January.

Chapter 20—God Satisfies Me With Long Life

1. This story from Colonel James E. Agnew was sent to the author through private correspondence.

Chapter 21—I Behold His Salvation

1. Strong, *Strong's Exhaustive Concordance of the Bible*, s.v. "salvation."

A PLACE OF TOTAL PROTECTION IN LIFE'S STORMS

978-1-59979-079-4 / $12.99

In a season of crisis and trouble, veteran Bible teacher Peggy Joyce Ruth presents real-life stories of God's sheild of protection, and what it means for you and those you love.

CHARISMA HOUSE